DE LIBRIS

PROSE AND VERSE

THE MACMILLAN COMPANY
NEW YORK · BOSTON · CHICAGO
ATLANTA · SAN FRANCISCO

MACMILLAN & CO., LIMITED
LONDON · BOMBAY · CALCUTTA
MELBOURNE

THE MACMILLAN CO. OF CANADA, LTD.
TORONTO

Venator? "Look! look! you may see all busy,
men and dogs, dogs and men, all busy."

THE OTTER HUNT IN THE "COMPLEAT ANGLER."

(From the original pen-drawing.)

DE LIBRIS

PROSE & VERSE

BY

AUSTIN DOBSON

Vt Mel Os, sic Cor Melos afficit, & reficit.
Deuteromelia.
A mixture of a *Song* doth ever adde Pleasure.
BACON (*adapted*).

New York
THE MACMILLAN COMPANY
1908

PROLOGUE

LECTOR BENEVOLE!—FOR SO
THEY USED TO CALL YOU, YEARS AGO,—
I CAN'T PRETEND TO MAKE YOU READ
THE PAGES THAT TO THIS SUCCEED;
NOR COULD I—IF I WOULD—EXCUSE
THE WAYWARD PROMPTINGS OF THE MUSE
AT WHOSE COMMAND I WROTE THEM DOWN.

I HAVE NO HOPE TO "PLEASE THE TOWN."
I DID BUT THINK SOME FRIENDLY SOUL
(NOT ILL-ADVISED, UPON THE WHOLE!)
MIGHT LIKE THEM; AND "TO INTERPOSE
A LITTLE EASE," BETWEEN THE PROSE,
SLIPPED IN THE SCRAPS OF VERSE, THAT THUS
THINGS MIGHT BE LESS MONOTONOUS.

THEN, *LECTOR,* BE *BENEVOLUS!*

[*The Author desires to express his thanks to Lord North-cliffe, Messrs. Macmillan and Co., Messrs. Smith, Elder and Co., Mr. William Heinemann, and Messrs. Virtue and Co., for kind permission to reprint those pieces in this volume concerning which no specific arrangements were made on their first appearance in type.*]

CONTENTS

PAGE

PROLOGUE v

ON SOME BOOKS AND THEIR ASSOCIATIONS . . . 1

AN EPISTLE TO AN EDITOR 17

BRAMSTON'S "MAN OF TASTE" 23

THE PASSIONATE PRINTER TO HIS LOVE 39

M. ROUQUET ON THE ARTS 43

THE FRIEND OF HUMANITY AND THE RHYMER . . . 65

THE PARENT'S ASSISTANT 69

A PLEASANT INVECTIVE AGAINST PRINTING 87

TWO MODERN BOOK ILLUSTRATORS—I. KATE GREENAWAY . 91

A SONG OF THE GREENAWAY CHILD 105

TWO MODERN BOOK ILLUSTRATORS—II. MR. HUGH THOMSON 109

HORATIAN ODE ON THE TERCENTENARY OF "DON QUIXOTE" . 125

THE BOOKS OF SAMUEL ROGERS 129

PEPYS' "DIARY" 147

A FRENCH CRITIC ON BATH 151

A WELCOME FROM THE "JOHNSON CLUB" 163

THACKERAY'S "ESMOND" 167

A MILTONIC EXERCISE 189

FRESH FACTS ABOUT FIELDING 193

THE HAPPY PRINTER 205

CROSS READINGS—AND CALEB WHITEFOORD . . . 209

THE LAST PROOF 221

INDEX 225

ILLUSTRATIONS

* THE OTTER HUNT IN THE "COMPLEAT ANGLER."
From an unpublished pen-drawing by Mr.
Hugh Thomson . . . . . *Frontispiece*

* GROUP OF CHILDREN. From the original pen-
drawing by Kate Greenaway for *The Library*,
1881 . . . . . . *To face p.* 93

* PENCIL-SKETCHES, by the same (No. 1) . . " 96

* PENCIL-SKETCH, by the same (No. 2) . . " 98

* PENCIL-SKETCHES, by the same (No. 3) . . " 100

* PENCIL-SKETCH, by the same (No. 4) . . " 102

THE BROWN BOOK-PLATE. From the original design
by Mr. Hugh Thomson in the possession of
Mr. Ernest Brown . . . . . " 111

* SIR ROGER DE COVERLEY AT THE ASSIZES. From a first
rough pencil-sketch, by the same, for *Days with
Roger de Coverley*, 1886 . . . . " 112

PEN-SKETCHES, by the same, on the Half-Title of
the *Ballad of Beau Brocade*, 1892. From the
originals in the possession of Mr. A. T. A.
Dobson . . . . " 114

* PEN-SKETCH (TRIPLET), by the same, on a Fly-leaf
of *Peg Woffington*, 1899 . . . " 116

EVELINA AND THE BRANGHTONS, by the same. From
the Cranford *Evelina*, 1903 . . . " 118

LADY CASTLEWOOD AND HER SON, by the same. From
the Cranford *Esmond*, 1905   .   .   . *To face p.* 120

MERCERY LANE, CANTERBURY, by the same. From
the original pencil-drawing for *Highways and
Byways in Kent*, 1907   .   .   .   .   "   122

*** *The originals of the illustrations preceded by an asterisk
are in the possession of the Author.*

ON SOME BOOKS AND THEIR
ASSOCIATIONS

ON SOME BOOKS AND THEIR
ASSOCIATIONS

NEW books can have few associations. They may
reach us on the best deckle-edged Whatman
paper, in the newest types of famous presses, with
backs of embossed vellum, with tasteful tasselled
strings,—and yet be no more to us than the constrained and uneasy acquaintances of yesterday.
Friends they may become to-morrow, the day after,
—perhaps *"hunc in annum et plures."* But for the
time being they have neither part nor lot in our past
of retrospect and suggestion. Of what we were, of
what we like or liked, they know nothing; and we—if
that be possible—know even less of them. Whether
familiarity will breed contempt, or whether they
will come home to our business and bosom,—these
are things that lie on the lap of the Fates.

But it is to be observed that the associations
of old books, as of new books, are not always

exclusively connected with their text or format,—are
sometimes, as a matter of fact, independent of both.
Often they are memorable to us by length of tenure,
by propinquity, — even by their patience under
neglect. We may never read them; and yet by
reason of some wholly external and accidental
characteristic, it would be a wrench to part with
them if the moment of separation—the inevitable
hour—should arrive at last. Here, to give an
instance in point, is a stained and battered French
folio, with patched corners,—Mons. N. Renouard's
translation of the *Metamorphoses d'Ovide*, 1637,
"enrichies de figures à chacune Fable" (very odd figures
some of them are!) and to be bought *"chez Pierre
Billaine, ruë Sainct Iacques, à la Bonne-Foy, deuant
S. Yues."* It has held no honoured place upon the
shelves; it has even resided *au rez-de-chaussée,*—that
is to say, upon the floor; but it is not less dear,—
not less desirable. For at the back of the "Dedication to the King" (Lewis XIII. to wit), is scrawled
in a slanting, irregular hand: *"Pour mademoiselle
de mons Son tres humble et tres obeissant Serviteur St.
André."* Between the fourth and fifth word, some
one, in a smaller writing of later date, has added
"par," and after "St. André," the signature
"Vandeuvre." In these irrelevant (and unsolicited)
interpolations, I take no interest. But who was
Mlle. de Mons? As Frederick Locker sings:

Did She live yesterday or ages back?
What colour were the eyes when bright and waking?
And were your ringlets fair, or brown, or black,
Poor little Head! that long has done with aching![1]

"Ages back" she certainly did *not* live, for the book is dated "1637," and "yesterday" is absurd. But that her eyes were bright,—nay, that they were particularly lively and vivacious, even as they are in the sanguine sketches of Antoine Watteau a hundred years afterwards, I am "confidous"—as Mrs. Slipslop would say. For my theory (in reality a foregone conclusion which I shrink from dispersing by any practical resolvent) is, that Mlle. de Mons was some delightful seventeenth-century French child, to whom the big volume had been presented as a picture-book. I can imagine the alert, straight-corsetted little figure, with ribboned hair, eagerly craning across the tall folio; and following curiously with her finger the legends under the copper "figures,"—"Narcisse en fleur," "Ascalaphe en hibou," "Jason endormant le dragon,"—and so forth, with much the same wonder that the Sinne-Beelden of Jacob Cats must have stirred

---

[1] This quatrain has the distinction of having been touched upon by Thackeray. When Mr. Locker's manuscript went to the *Cornhill Magazine* in 1860, it ran thus:

Did she live yesterday, or ages sped?
What colour were the eyes when bright and waking?
And were your ringlets fair? Poor little head!
—Poor little heart! that long has done with aching.

in the little Dutchwomen of Middleburgh. There can be no Mlle. de Mons but this,—and for me she can never grow old!

Sometimes it comes to pass that the association is of a more far-fetched and fanciful kind. In the great Ovid it lies in an inscription: in my next case it is "another-guess" matter. The folio this time is the *Sylva Sylvarum* of the "Right Hon. Francis Lo. Verulam, Viscount St. Alban," of whom some people still prefer to speak as Lord Bacon. 'Tis only the "sixt Edition"; but it was to be bought at the Great Turk's Head, "next to the Mytre Tauerne" (not the modern pretender, be it observed!), which is in itself a feature of interest. A former possessor, from his notes, appears to have been largely preoccupied with that ignoble clinging to life which so exercised Matthew Arnold, for they relate chiefly to laxative simples for medicine; and he comforts himself, in April, 1695, by transcribing Bacon's reflection that "a Life led in *Religion* and in *Holy Exercises*" conduces to longevity,—an aphorism which, however useful as an argument for length of days, is a rather remote reason for religion. But what to me is always most seductive in the book is, that to this edition (not copy, of course) of 1651 Master Izaak Walton, when he came, in his *Compleat Angler* of 1653, to discuss such abstract questions as the transmission of sound under water, and the ages of carp and pike, must probably have referred. He often mentions "Sir Francis Bacon's" *History of Life and Death,* which is included in the volume. No doubt it would be more reasonable and more "congruous" that Bacon's book should suggest Bacon. But there it is. That illogical "succession of ideas" which puzzled my Uncle Toby, invariably recalls to me, not the imposing folio to be purchased "next to the Mytre Tauerne" in Fleet Street, but the unpretentious eighteenpenny octavo which, two years later, was on sale at Richard Marriot's in St. Dunstan's churchyard hard by, and did no more than borrow its erudition from the riches of the Baconian storehouse.

Life, and its prolongation, is again the theme of the next book (also mentioned, by the way, in Walton) which I take up, though unhappily it has no inscription. It is a little old calf-clad copy of Lewis Cornaro's *Sure and Certain Methods of attaining a Long and Healthful Life,* 4th ed., 24mo, 1727; and was bought at the Bewick sale of February, 1884, as having once belonged to Robert Elliot Bewick, only son of the famous old Newcastle wood-engraver. As will be shown later, it is easy to be misled in these matters, but I cannot help believing that this volume, which looks as if it had been re-bound, is the one Thomas Bewick mentions in his *Memoir* as having been his companion in those speculative wanderings over the Town Moor or the Elswick Fields, when, as an apprentice, he planned his future *à la* Franklin and devised schemes for his conduct in life. In attaining Cornaro's tale of years he did not succeed; though he seems to have faithfully practised the periods of abstinence enjoined (but probably not observed) by another of the "noble Venetian's" professed admirers, Mr. Addison of the *Spectator*.

If I have admitted a momentary misgiving as to the authenticity of the foregoing relic of the "father of white line," there can be none about the next item to which I now come. Once, on a Westminster bookstall, long since disappeared, I found a copy of a seventh edition of the *Pursuits of Literature* of T. J. Mathias, Queen Charlotte's Treasurer's Clerk. Brutally cut down by the binder, that *durus arator* had unexpectedly spared a solitary page for its manuscript comment, which was thoughtfully turned up and folded in. It was a note to this couplet in Mathias, his Dialogue II.:—

> From Bewick's magick wood throw borrow'd rays
> O'er many a page in gorgeous Bulmer's blaze,—

"gorgeous Bulmer" (the epithet is over-colored!) being the William Bulmer who, in 1795, issued the *Poems of Goldsmith and Parnell*. "I" (says the writer of the note) "was chiefly instrumental to this ingenious artist's [Bewick's] excellence in this art. I first initiated his master, Mr. Ra. Beilby (of Newcastle) into the art, and his first essay was the execution of the cuts in my Treatise on Mensuration, printed in 4to, 1770. Soon after I recommended the same artist to execute the cuts to Dr. Horsley's edition of the works of Newton. Accordingly Mr. B. had the job, who put them into the hands of his assistant, Mr. Bewick, who executed them as his first work in wood, and that in a most elegant manner, tho' spoiled in the printing by John Nichols, the Black-letter printer. C. H. 1798."

"C. H." is Dr. Charles Hutton, the Woolwich mathematician. His note is a little in the vaunting vein of that "founder of fortun's," the excellent Uncle Pumblechook of *Great Expectations,* for his services scarcely amounted to "initiating" Bewick or his master into the art of engraving on wood. Moreover, his memory must have failed him, for Bewick, and not Beilby, did the majority of the cuts to the *Mensuration,* including a much-praised diagram of the tower of St. Nicholas Church at Newcastle, afterwards a familiar object in the younger man's designs and tail-pieces. Be this as it may, Dr. Hutton's note was surely worth rescuing from the ruthless binder's plough.

Between the work of Thomas Bewick and the work of Samuel Pepys, it is idle to attempt any ingenious connecting link, save the fact that they both wrote autobiographically. The "Pepys" in question here, however, is not the famous *Diary*, but the Secretary to the Admiralty's "only other acknowledged work," namely, the privately printed *Memoires Relating to the State of the Royal Navy of England, for Ten Years,* 1690; and this copy may undoubtedly lay claim to exceptional interest. For not only does it comprise those manuscript corrections in the author's handwriting, which Dr. Tanner reproduced in his excellent Clarendon Press reprint of last year, but it includes the two portrait plates by Robert White after Kneller. The larger is bound in as a frontispiece; the smaller (the ex-libris) is inserted at the beginning. The main attraction of the book to me, however, is its previous owners—one especially. My immediate predecessor was a well-known collector, Professor Edward Solly, at whose sale in 1886 I bought it; and he in his turn had acquired it in 1877, at Dr. Rimbault's sale. Probably what drew us all to the little volume was not so much its disclosure of the lamentable state of the Caroline navy, and of the monstrous toadstools that flourished so freely in the ill-ventilated holds of His Majesty's ships-of-war, as the fact that it had once belonged to that brave old philanthropist, Captain Thomas Coram of the Foundling Hospital. To him it was presented in March, 1724, by one C. Jackson; and he afterwards handed it on to a

Mr. Mills. Pasted at the end is Coram's autograph letter, dated "June 10th, 1746." "To Mr. Mills These. Worthy Sir I happend to find among my few Books, Mr. Pepys his memoires, wch I thought might be acceptable to you & therefore pray you to accept of it. I am wth much Respect Sir your most humble Ser^{t.} THOMAS CORAM."

At the Foundling Hospital is a magnificent full-length of Coram, with curling white locks and kindly, weather-beaten face, from the brush of his friend and admirer, William Hogarth. It is to Hogarth and his fellow-Governor at the Foundling, John Wilkes, that my next jotting relates. These strange colleagues in charity afterwards—as is well known—quarrelled bitterly over politics. Hogarth caricatured Wilkes in the *Times*: Wilkes replied by a *North Briton* article (No. 17) so scurrilous and malignant that Hogarth was stung into rejoining with that famous squint-eyed semblance of his former crony, which has handed him down to posterity more securely than the portraits of Zoffany and Earlom. Wilkes's action upon this was to reprint his article with the addition of a bulbous-nosed woodcut of Hogarth "from the Life." These facts lent interest to an entry which for years had been familiar to me in the Sale Catalogue of Mr. H. P. Standly, and which ran thus: "The NORTH BRITON, No. 17, with a PORTRAIT of HOGARTH in WOOD; *and a severe*

critique on some of his works: in Ireland's handwriting
is the following—'*This paper was given to me by Mrs.*
Hogarth, Aug. 1782, *and is the identical North Briton*
purchased by Hogarth, and carried in his pocket many
days to show his friends.' " The Ireland referred to
(as will presently appear) was Samuel Ireland of
the *Graphic Illustrations*. When, in 1892, dispersed
items of the famous Joly collection began to
appear sporadically in the second-hand catalogues,
I found in that of a well-known London bookseller
an entry plainly describing this one, and proclaiming
that it came "from the celebrated collection of Mr.
Standly, of St. Neots." Unfortunately, the scrap
of paper connecting it with Mrs. Hogarth's present
to Ireland had been destroyed. Nevertheless, I
secured my prize, had it fittingly bound up with
the original number which accompanied it; and
here and there, in writing about Hogarth, bragged
consequentially about my fortunate acquisition.
Then came a day—a day to be marked with a black
stone!—when in the British Museum Print Room,
and looking through the "—— Collection," for the
moment deposited there, I came upon *another* copy
of the *North Briton,* bearing in Samuel Ireland's
writing a notification to the effect that it was the
identical No. 17, etc., etc. Now which is the right
one? Is either the right one? I inspect mine
distrustfully. It is soiled, and has evidently been

folded; it is scribbled with calculations; it has all
the aspect of a *vénérable vétusté*. That it came from
the Standly collection, I am convinced. But that
other pretender in the (now dispersed) "—— Collection"? And was not Samuel Ireland (*nomen invisum!*)
the, if not fraudulent, at least too-credulous father
of one William Henry Ireland, who, at eighteen,
wrote *Vortigern and Rowena,* and palmed it off as
genuine Shakespeare? I fear me—I much fear me—
that, in the words of the American showman, I have
been "weeping over the wrong grave."

To prolong these vagrant adversaria would not
be difficult. Here, for example, dated 1779, are
the *Coplas* of the poet Don Jorge Manrique, which,
having no Spanish, I am constrained to study in
the renderings of Longfellow. Don Jorge was
a Spaniard of the Spaniards, Commendador of
Montizon, Knight of the Order of Santiago, Captain
of a company in the Guards of Castile, and withal
a valiant *soldado,* who died of a wound received in
battle. But the attraction of my volume is, that,
at the foot of the title-page, in beautiful neat script,
appear the words, "Robert Southey. Paris. 17 May
1817,"—being the year in which Southey stayed
at Como with Walter Savage Landor. Here are
the *Works* of mock-heroic John Philips, 1720,
whose *Blenheim* the Tories pitted against Addison's
Campaign, and whose *Splendid Shilling* still shines

lucidly among eighteenth-century parodies. This
copy bears—also on the title-page—the autograph of
James Thomson, not yet the author of *The Seasons*;
and includes the book-plate of Lord Prestongrange,
—that "Lord Advocate Grant" of whom you may
read in the *Kidnapped* of "R. L. S." Here again is
an edition (the first) of Hazlitt's *Lectures on the
English Comic Writers*, annotated copiously in MS.
by a contemporary reader who was certainly not an
admirer; and upon whom W. H.'s cockneyisms,
Gallicisms, egotisms, and "*ille*-isms" generally, seem
to have had the effect of a red rag upon an inveterately
insular bull. "A very ingenious but pert, dogmatical,
and Prejudiced Writer" is his uncomplimentary
addition to the author's name. Then here is
Cunningham's *Goldsmith* of 1854, vol. i., castigated
with equal energy by that Alaric Alexander Watts,[1]
of whose egregious strictures upon Wordsworth we
read not long since in the *Cornhill Magazine*, and
who will not allow Goldsmith to say, in the *Haunch
of Venison*, "the porter and eatables followed behind."
"They could scarcely have followed before,"—he
objects, in the very accents of Boeotia. Nor will
he pass "the hollow-sounding bittern" of the
Deserted Village. A barrel may sound hollow, but

---

[1] So he was christened. But Lockhart chose to insist that his second
prename should properly be "Attila," and thenceforth he was spoken of in
this way.

not a bird—this wiseacre acquaints us. Had the
gifted author of *Lyrics of the Heart* never heard of
rhetorical figures? But he is not Goldsmith's only
hyper-critic. Charles Fox, who admired *The Traveller,*
thought Olivia's famous song in the *Vicar* "foolish,"
and added that "folly" was a bad rhyme to "melancholy."[1] He must have forgotten Milton's :—

> Bird that shunn'st the noise of folly,
> Most musicall, most melancholy!

Or he might have gone to the other camp, and
remembered Pope on Mrs. Howard :—

> Not warp'd by Passion, aw'd by Rumour,
> Not grave thro' Pride, or gay thro' Folly,
> An equal Mixture of good Humour,
> And sensible soft Melancholy.

---

[1] *Recollections,* by Samuel Rogers, 2nd ed. 1859, 43.

AN EPISTLE TO AN EDITOR

AN EPISTLE TO AN EDITOR

"Jamais les arbres verts n'ont essayé d'être bleus."—
                                                    THÉOPHILE GAUTIER

"A NEW Review!" You make me tremble
(Though as to that, I can dissemble
Till I hear more). But is it "new"?
And will it be a *real* Review?—
I mean, a Court wherein the scales
Weigh equally both him that fails,
And him that hits the mark?—a place
Where the accus'd can plead his case,
If wrong'd? All this I need to know
Before I (arrogant!) say "Go."

"We, that are very old" (the phrase
Is STEELE'S, not mine!), in former days,
Have seen so many "new Reviews"
Arise, arraign, absolve, abuse;—
Proclaim their mission to the top
(Where there's still room!), then slowly drop,

Shrink down, fade out, and *sans* preferment,
Depart to their obscure interment;—
We should be pardon'd if we doubt
That a new venture *can* hold out.

It *will*, you say. Then don't be "new";
Be "old." The Old is still the True.
Nature (said GAUTIER) never tries
To alter her accustom'd dyes;
And all your novelties at best
Are ancient puppets, newly drest.
What you must do, is not to shrink
From speaking out the thing you think;
And blaming where 'tis right to blame,
Despite tradition and a Name.
Yet don't expand a trifling blot,
Or ban the book for what it's not
(That is the poor device of those
Who cavil where they can't oppose!);
Moreover (this is *very* old!),
Be courteous—even when you scold!

Blame I put first, but not at heart.
You must give Praise the foremost part;—
Praise that to those who write is breath
Of Life, if just; if unjust, Death.
Praise then the things that men revere;
Praise what they love, not what they fear;

Praise too the young; praise those who try;
Praise those who fail, but by and by
May do good work.   Those who succeed,
You'll praise perforce,—so there's no need
To speak of that.   And as to each,
See you keep measure in your speech;—
See that your praise be so exprest
That the best man shall get the best;
Nor fail of the fit word you meant
Because your epithets are spent.
Remember that our language gives
No limitless superlatives;
And SHAKESPEARE, HOMER, *should* have more
Than the last knocker at the door!

"We, that are very old!"—May this
Excuse the hint you find amiss.
My thoughts, I feel, are what to-day
Men call *vieux jeu*.   Well!—"let them say."
The Old, at least, we know: the New
(A changing Shape that all pursue!)
Has been,—may be, a fraud.
                              —But there!
Wind to your sail!   *Vogue la galère!*

BRAMSTON'S "MAN OF TASTE"

BRAMSTON'S "MAN OF TASTE"

WERE you to inquire respectfully of the infallible critic (if such indeed there be!) for the source of the aphorism, "Music has charms to soothe a savage beast," he would probably "down" you contemptuously in the Johnsonian fashion by replying that you had "just enough of learning to misquote";— that the last word was notoriously "breast" and not "beast";—and that the line, as Macaulay's, and every Board School-boy besides must be abundantly aware, is to be found in Congreve's tragedy of *The Mourning Bride*. But he would be wrong; and, in fact, would only be confirming the real author's contention that "Sure, of all blockheads, *Scholars* are the worst." For, whether connected with Congreve or not, the words are correctly given; and they occur in the Rev. James Bramston's satire, *The Man of Taste*, 1733, running in a couplet as follows:—

> Musick has charms to sooth a savage beast,
> And therefore proper at a Sheriff's feast.

Moreover, according to the handbooks, this is not the only passage from a rather obscure original which has held its own. "Without black-velvet-britches, what is man?"—is another (a speculation which might have commended itself to Don Quixote);[1] while *The Art of Politicks,* also by Bramston, contains a third:—

> What's not destroy'd by Time's devouring Hand?
> Where's *Troy,* and where's the *May-Pole* in the *Strand*?

Polonius would perhaps object against a "devouring hand." But the survival of—at least—three fairly current citations from a practically forgotten minor Georgian satirist would certainly seem to warrant a few words upon the writer himself, and his chief performance in verse.

The Rev. James Bramston was born in 1694 or 1695 at Skreens, near Chelmsford, in Essex, his father, Francis Bramston, being the fourth son of Sir Moundeford Bramston, Master in Chancery, whose father again was Sir John Bramston, Lord Chief Justice of the King's Bench, generally known as "the elder."[2] James Bramston was admitted to Westminster School in 1708. In 1713 he became a

---

[1] Whose *grande tenue* or holiday wear—Cervantes tells us—was "a doublet of fine cloth and *velvet breeches* and shoes to match" (ch. 1).

[2] Sir John Bramston, the younger, was the author of the "watery incoherent *Autobiography*"—as Carlyle calls it—published by the Camden Society in 1845.

scholar at Christ Church, Oxford, proceeding B.A.
in 1717, and M.A. in 1720. In 1723 he was
made Vicar of Lurgashall, and in 1725 of Harting,
both of which Sussex livings he held until his death
in March 1744, ten weeks before the death of Pope.
His first published verses (1715) were on Dr.
Radcliffe. In 1729 he printed the *Art of Politicks*,
one of the many contemporary imitations of the *Ars
Poetica*; and in 1733 *The Man of Taste*. He also
wrote a mediocre variation on the *Splendid Shilling* of
John Philips, entitled the *Crooked Sixpence,* 1743.
Beyond a statement in Dallaway's *Sussex* that "he
[Bramston] was a man of original humour, the fame
and proofs of whose colloquial wit are still remembered"; and the supplementary information that, as
incumbent of Lurgashall, he received an annual *modus*
of a fat buck and doe from the neighbouring
Park of Petworth, nothing more seems to have been
recorded of him.

The Crooked Sixpence is, at best, an imitation of an
imitation; and as a Miltonic *pastiche* does not excel
that of Philips, or rival the more serious *Lewesdon
Hill* of Crowe. *The Art of Politicks,* in its turn,
would need a fairly long commentary to make
what is only moderately interesting moderately
intelligible, while eighteenth-century copies of
Horace's letter to the Pisos are "plentiful as
blackberries." But *The Man of Taste,* based, as

it is, on the presentment of a never extinct type, the connoisseur against Nature *invitissima Minerva*, is still worthy of passing notice.

In the sub-title of the poem, it is declared to be "Occasion'd by an Epistle of Mr. Pope's on that Subject [*i.e.* "Taste"]. This was what is now known as No. 4 of the *Moral Essays,* "On the Use of Riches." But its first title in 1731 was "Of Taste"; and this was subsequently altered to "Of False Taste." It was addressed to Pope's friend, Richard Boyle, Earl of Burlington; and, under the style of "Timon's Villa," employed, for its chief illustration of wasteful and vacuous magnificence, the ostentatious seat which James Brydges, first Duke of Chandos, had erected at Canons, near Edgware. The story of Pope's epistle does not belong to this place. But in the print of *The Man of Taste,* William Hogarth, gratifying concurrently a personal antipathy, promptly attacked Pope, Burlington, and his own *bête noire,* Burlington's architect, William Kent. Pope, to whom Burlington acts as hodman, is depicted whitewashing Burlington Gate, Piccadilly, which is labelled "Taste," and over which rises Kent's statue, subserviently supported at the angles of the pediment by Raphael and Michelangelo. In his task, the poet, a deformed figure in a tye-wig, bountifully bespatters the passers-by, particularly the chariot of the Duke of Chandos. The satire was not very brilliant or ingenious; but its meaning was clear.   Pope was prudent enough to make no reply; though, as Mr. G. S. Layard shows in his *Suppressed Plates,* it seems that the print was, or was sought to be, called in by those concerned.   Bramston's poem, which succeeded in 1733, does not enter into the quarrel, it may be because of the anger aroused by the pictorial reply.   But if—as announced on its title-page,—it was suggested by Pope's epistle, it would also seem to have borrowed its name from Hogarth's caricature.

It was first issued in folio by Pope's publisher, Lawton Gilliver of Fleet Street, and has a frontispiece engraved by Gerard Vandergucht.   This depicts a wide-skirted, effeminate-looking personage, carrying a long cane with a head fantastically carved, and surrounded by various objects of art.   In the background rises what is apparently intended for the temple of a formal garden; and behind this again, a winged ass capers skittishly upon the summit of Mount Helicon.   As might be anticipated, the poem is in the heroic measure of Pope.   But though many of its couplets are compact and pointed, Bramston has not yet learned from his model the art of varying his pausation, and the period closes his second line with the monotony of a minute gun.   Another defect, noticed by Warton, is that the speaker throughout is made to profess the errors satirised, and to be the unabashed mouth-piece of his own fatuity. "Mine," say the concluding lines,—

> Mine are the gallant Schemes of Politesse,
> For books, and buildings, politicks, and dress.
> This is *True Taste,* and whoso likes it not,
> Is blockhead, coxcomb, puppy, fool, and sot.

One is insensibly reminded of a quotation from P. L. Courier, made in the *Cornhill* many years since by the once famous "Jacob Omnium" when replying controversially to the author of *Ionica.* "*Je vois*"— says Courier, after recapitulating a string of abusive epithets hurled at him by his opponent—"*je vois ce qu'il veut dire: il entend que lui et moi sont d'avis different; et c'est là sa manière de s'exprimer.*" It was also the manner of our Man of Taste.

The second line of the above quotation from Bramston gives us four of the things upon which his hero lays down the law. Let us see what he says about literature. As a professing critic he prefers books with notes:—

> Tho' *Blackmore's* works my soul with raptures fill,
> With notes by *Bently* they'd be better still.

Swift he detests—not of course for detestable qualities, but because he is so universally admired. In poetry he holds by rhyme as opposed to blank verse:—

> Verse without rhyme I never could endure,
> Uncouth in numbers, and in sense obscure.

To him as Nature, when he ceas'd to see,
Milton's an *universal Blank* to me. . .
Thompson [*sic*] write blank, but know that for that reason
These lines shall live, when thine are out of season.
Rhyme binds and beautifies the Poet's lays
As *London* Ladies owe their shape to stays.

In this the Man of Taste is obviously following the reigning fashion. But if we may assume Bramston himself to approve what his hero condemns, he must have been in advance of his age, for blank verse had but sparse advocates at this time, or for some time to come. Neither Gray, nor Johnson, nor Goldsmith were ever reconciled to what the last of them styles "this unharmonious measure." Goldsmith, in particular, would probably have been in exact agreement with the couplet as to the controlling powers of rhyme, "If rhymes, therefore," he writes, in the *Enquiry into Polite Learning,*[1] "be more difficult [than blank verse], for that very reason, I would have our poets write in rhyme. Such a restriction upon the thought of a good poet, often lifts and encreases the vehemence of every sentiment; for fancy, like a fountain, plays highest by diminishing the aperture."[2]

The Man of Taste's idol, in matters dramatic, is

[1] Ed. 1759, p. 151.
[2] Montaigne has a somewhat similar illustration: "As *Cleanthes* said, that as the voice being forciblie pent in the narrow gullet of a trumpet, at last issueth forth more strong ·and shriller, so me seemes, that a sentence cunningly and closely couched in measure-keeping Posie, darts it selfe forth more furiously, and wounds me even to the quicke" (*Essayes,* bk. i. ch. xxv. (Florio's translation).

Colley Cibber, who, however, deserves the laurel he wears, not for *The Careless Husband,* his best comedy, but for his Epilogues and other Plays.

> It pleases me, that *Pope* unlaurell'd goes,
> While *Cibber* wears the Bays for Play-house Prose.
> So *Britain's* Monarch once uncover'd sate,
> While *Bradshaw* bully'd in a broad-brimmed hat,—

a reminiscence of King Charles's trial which might have been added to Bramston stock quotations. The productions of "Curll's chaste press" are also this connoisseur's favourite reading,—the lives of players in particular, probably on the now obsolete grounds set forth in Carlyle's essay on Scott.[1] Among these the memoirs of Cibber's "Lady Betty Modish," Mrs. Oldfield, then lately dead, and buried in Westminster Abbey, are not obscurely indicated.

In morals our friend—as might be expected *circa* 1730—is a Freethinker and Deist. Tindal is his text-book: his breviary the *Fable of the Bees:*—

> T' improve in Morals *Mandevil* I read,
> And *Tyndal's* Scruples are my settled Creed.
> I travell'd early, and I soon saw through
> Religion all, e'er I was twenty-two.
> Shame, Pain, or Poverty shall I endure,
> When ropes or opium can my ease procure?
> When money's gone, and I no debts can pay,
> Self-murder is an honourable way.

---

[1] "It has been said, 'There are no English lives worth reading except those of Players, who by the nature of the case have bidden Respectability good-day.'"

> As *Pasaran* directs I'd end my life,
> And kill myself, my daughter, and my wife.

He would, of course, have done nothing of the kind; nor, for the matter of that, did his Piedmontese preceptor.[1]

Nil admirari is the motto of the Man of Taste in Building, where he is naturally at home. He can see no symmetry in the Banqueting House, or in St. Paul's Covent Garden, or even in St. Paul's itself.

> Sure wretched *Wren* was taught by bungling *Jones,*
> To murder mortar, and disfigure stones!

"Substantial" Vanbrugh he likes—chiefly because his work would make "such noble ruins." Cost is his sole criterion, and here he, too, seems to glance obliquely at Canons:—

> *Dorick, Ionick,* shall not there be found,
> But it shall cost me threescore thousand pound.

But this was moderate, as the Edgware "folly" reached £250,000. In Gardening he follows the latest whim for landscape. Here is his burlesque of the principles of Bridgeman and Batty Langley:—

> Does it not merit the beholder's praise,
> What's high to sink? and what is low to raise?

---

[1] Count Passeran was a freethinking nobleman who wrote *A Philosophical Discourse on Death,* in which he defended suicide, though he refrained from resorting to it himself. Pope refers to him in the *Epilogue to the Satires,* Dialogue i. 124:—

> If Blount despatch'd himself, he play'd the man,
> And so may'st thou, illustrious Passeran!

D

Slopes shall ascend where once a green-house stood,
And in my horse-pond I will plant a wood.
Let misers dread the hoarded gold to waste,
Expence and alteration show a *Taste*.

As a connoisseur of Painting this enlightened virtuoso is given over to Hogarth's hated dealers in the Black Masters:—

In curious paintings I'm exceeding nice,
And know their several beauties by their *Price*.
Auctions and *Sales* I constantly attend,
But chuse my pictures by a *skilful Friend*.
Originals and copics much the same,
The Picture's value is the *painter's name*.[1]

Of Sculpture he says—

In spite of *Addison* and ancient *Rome*,
Sir *Cloudesly Shovel's* is my fav'rite tomb.[2]
How oft have I with admiration stood,
To view some City-magistrate in wood?
I gaze with pleasure on a Lord May'r's head
Cast with propriety in gilded lead,—

the allusion being obviously to Cheere's manufactory of such popular garden decorations at Hyde Park Corner.

In Coins and Medals, true to his instinct for liking

---

[1] See *post*, "M. Rouquet on the Arts," p. 51.

[2] "Sir *Cloudesly Shovel's* Monument has very often given me great Offence: Instead of the brave rough English Admiral, which was the distinguishing Character of that plain, gallant Man, he is represented on his Tomb [in Westminster Abbey] by the Figure of a Beau, dressed in a long Perriwig, and reposing himself upon Velvet Cushions under a Canopy of State" (*Spectator*, March 30, 1711).

the worst the best, he prefers the modern to the antique. In Music, with Hogarth's Rake two years later, he is all for that "Dagon of the nobility and gentry," imported song:—

> Without *Italian,* or without an ear,
> To *Bononcini's* musick I adhere;—

though he confesses to a partiality for the bagpipe on the ground that your true Briton "loves a grumbling noise," and he favours organs and the popular oratorios. But his "top talent is a bill of fare":—

> Sir Loins and rumps of beef offend my eyes,[1]
> Pleas'd with frogs fricass[e]ed, and coxcomb-pies.
> Dishes I chuse though little, yet genteel,
> *Snails*[2] the first course, and *Peepers*[3] crown the meal.
> Pigs heads with hair on, much my fancy please,
> I love young colly-flowers if stew'd in cheese,
> And give ten guineas for a pint of peas!
> No tatling servants to my table come,
> My Grace is *Silence,* and my waiter *Dumb.*

He is not without his aspirations.

> Could I the *privilege* of *Peer* procure,
> The rich I'd bully, and oppress the poor.
> To *give* is wrong, but it is wronger still,
> On any terms to *pay* a tradesman's bill.

---

[1] As they did those of Goldsmith's "Beau Tibbs." "I hate your immense loads of meat . . . extreme disgusting to those who are in the least acquainted with high life" (*Citizen of the World,* 1762, i. 241).

[2] The edible or Roman snail (*Helix pomatia*) is still known to continental cuisines—and gipsy camps. It was introduced into England as an epicure's dish in the seventeenth century.

[3] Young chickens.

I'd make the insolent Mechanicks stay,
And keep my ready-money all for *play*.
I'd try if any pleasure could be found
In *tossing-up* for twenty thousand pound.
Had I whole Counties, I to *White's* would go,
And set lands, woods, and rivers at a throw.
But should I meet with an unlucky run,
And at a throw be gloriously undone;
My *debts of honour* I'd discharge the first,
Let all my *lawful creditors* be curst.

Here he perfectly exemplifies that connexion between connoisseurship and play which Fielding discovers in Book xiii. of *Tom Jones*.[1] An anecdote of C. J. Fox aptly exhibits the final couplet in action, and proves that fifty years later, at least, the same convenient code was in operation. Fox once won about eight thousand pounds at cards. Thereupon an eager creditor promptly presented himself, and pressed for payment. "Impossible, Sir," replied Fox, "I must first discharge my debts of honour." The creditor expostulated. "Well, Sir, give me your bond." The bond was delivered to Fox, who tore it up and flung the pieces into the fire. "Now, Sir," said he, "my debt to you is a debt of honour," and immediately paid him.[2]

---

[1] "But the science of gaming is that which above all others employs their thoughts [*i.e.* the thoughts of the 'young gentlemen of our times']. These are the studies of their graver hours, while for their amusements they have the vast circle of connoisseurship, painting, music, statuary, and natural philosophy, or rather *unnatural*, which deals in the wonderful, and knows nothing of nature, except her monsters and imperfections" (ch. v.).

[2] *Table-Talk of Samuel Rogers* [by Dyce], 1856, p. 73.

But we must abridge our levies on Pope's imitator. In Dress the Man of Taste's aim seems to have been to emulate his own footman, and at this point comes in the already quoted reference to velvet "inexpressibles"—(a word which, the reader may be interested to learn, is as old as 1793). His "pleasures," as might be expected, like those of Goldsmith's Switzers, "are but low"—

> To boon companions I my time would give,
> With players, pimps, and parasites I'd live.
> I would with *Jockeys* from *Newmarket* dine,
> And to *Rough-riders* give my choicest wine. . .
> My ev'nings all I would with *sharpers* spend,
> And make the *Thief-catcher* my bosom friend.
> In *Fig*, the Prize-fighter, by day delight,
> And sup with *Colly Cibber* ev'ry night.

At which point—and probably in his cups—we leave our misguided fine gentleman of 1733, doubtless a fair sample of many of his class under the second George, and not wholly unknown under that monarch's successors—even to this hour. *Le jour va passer; mais la folie ne passera pas!*

A parting quotation may serve to illustrate one of those changes of pronunciation which have taken place in so many English words. Speaking of his villa, or country-box, the Man of Taste says—

> *Pots* o'er the door I'll place like Cits balconies,
> Which *Bently* calls the *Gardens of Adonis*.

To make this a peg for a dissertation on the jars
of lettuce and fennel grown by the Greeks for the
annual Adonis festivals, is needless. But it may be
noted that Bramston, with those of his day,—Swift
excepted,—scans the "o" in balcony long, a practice
which continued far into the nineteenth century.
"Cóntemplate," said Rogers, "is bad enough; but
balcŏny makes me sick."[1]   And even in 1857, two
years after Rogers's death, the late Frederick Locker,
writing of *Piccadilly*, speaks of "Old Q's" well-
known window in that thoroughfare as "Primrose
balcŏny."

Table-Talk, 1856, p. 248.

THE PASSIONATE PRINTER TO
HIS LOVE

THE PASSIONATE PRINTER TO
HIS LOVE

(*Whose name is Amanda*)

With Apologies to the Shade of Christopher Marlowe

COME live with me and be my Dear;
    And till that happy bond shall lapse,
I'll set your Poutings in *Brevier*,[1]
    Your Praises in the largest CAPS.

There's *Diamond*—'tis for your Eyes;
    There's *Ruby*—that will match your Lips;
Pearl, for your Teeth; and *Minion*-size
    To suit your dainty Finger-tips.

In *Nonpareil* I'll put your Face;
    In *Rubric* shall your Blushes rise;
There is no *Bourgeois* in *your* Case;
    Your *Form* can never need "*Revise*."

Your Cheek seems "*Ready for the Press*";
    Your Laugh as *Clarendon* is clear;
There's more distinction in your Dress
    Than in the oldest *Elzevir*.

[1] "Pronounced Bre-veer" (Printers' Vocabulary).

So with me live, and with me die;
　　And may no "FINIS" e'er intrude
To break into mere "*Printers' Pie*"
　　The Type of our Beatitude!

(ERRATUM.—If my suit you flout,
　　And choose some happier Youth to wed,
'Tis but to cross AMANDA out,
　　And read another name instead.)

M. ROUQUET ON THE ARTS

M. ROUQUET ON THE ARTS

M. ROUQUET's book is a rare duodecimo of some two hundred pages, bound in sheep, which, in the copy before us, has reached that particular stage of disintegration when the scarfskin, without much persuasion, peels away in long strips. Its title is— *L'État des Arts, en Angleterre. Par M. Rouquet, de l'Académie Royale de Peinture & de Sculpture*; and it is *"imprimé à Paris,"* though it was to be obtained from John Nourse, *"Libraire dans le* Strand, *proche* Temple-barr"—a well-known importer of foreign books, and one of Henry Fielding's publishers. The date is 1755, being the twenty-eighth year of the reign of His Majesty King George the Second—a reign not generally regarded as favourable to art of any kind. In what month of 1755 the little volume was first put forth does not appear; but it must have been before October, when Nourse issued an English version. There is a dedication, in the approved French fashion, to the Marquis de Marigny, *"Directeur & Ordonnateur Général de ses Bâtimens, Jardins, Arts, Académies & Manufactures"* to Lewis

the Fifteenth, above which is a delicate headpiece
by M. Charles-Nicolas Cochin (the greatest of the
family), where a couple of that artist's well-nourished
amorini, insecurely attached to festoons, distribute
palms and laurels in vacuity under a coroneted
oval displaying fishes. For Monsieur Abel-François
Poisson, Marquis de Marigny at de Ménars, was
the younger brother of Jeanne-Antoinette Poisson,
the celebrated Marquise de Pompadour. Cochin's
etching is dated "1754"; and the "Approbation"
at the end of the volume bears his signature in his
capacity of *Censeur.*

Of the "M. Rouquet" of the title-page biography
tells us little; but it may be well, before speaking
of his book, to bring that little together. He was
a Swiss Protestant of French extraction, born at
Geneva in 1702. His Christian names were Jean-
André; and he had come to England from his
native land towards the close of the reign of George
the First. Many of his restless compatriots also
sought these favoured shores. Labelye, who rose
from a barber's shop to be the architect of London
Bridge; Liotard, once regarded as a rival of
Reynolds; Michael Moser, eventually Keeper of
the Royal Academy, had all migrated from the
"stormy mansions" where, in the words of Goldsmith's philosophic Wanderer—

Winter ling'ring chills the lap of May.

Like Moser, Rouquet was a chaser and an enameller.
He lodged on the south side of Leicester Fields,
in a house afterwards the residence of another
Switzer of the same craft, that miserable Theodore
Gardelle, who in 1761 murdered his landlady, Mrs.
King. Of Rouquet's activities as an artist in
England there are scant particulars. The ordinary
authorities affirm that he imitated and rivalled the
popular miniaturist and enameller, Christian Zincke,
who retired from practice in 1746; and he is loosely
described as "the companion of Hogarth, Garrick,
Foote, and the wits of the day." Of his relations
with Foote and Garrick there is scant record; but
with Hogarth, his near neighbour in the Fields,
he was certainly well acquainted, since in 1746 he
prepared explanations in French for a number of
Hogarth's prints. These took the form of letters
to a friend in Paris, and are supposed to have been,
if not actually inspired, at least approved by the
painter. They usually accompanied all the sets of
Hogarth's engravings which went abroad; and,
according to George Steevens, it was Hogarth's
intention ultimately to have them translated and
enlarged. Rouquet followed these a little later by
a separate description of "The March to Finchley,"
designed specially for the edification of Marshal
Foucquet de Belle-Isle, who, when the former letters
had been written, was a prisoner of war at Windsor.

In a brief introduction to this last, the author, hitherto unnamed, is spoken of as *"Mr. Rouquet, connu par ses Ouvrages d'Émail."*

After thirty years' sojourn in this country, Rouquet transferred himself to Paris. At what precise date he did this is not stated, but by a letter to Hogarth from the French capital, printed by John Ireland, the original of which is in the British Museum, he was there, and had been there several months, in March 1753. The letter gives a highly favourable account of its writer's fortunes. Business is "coming in very smartly," he says. He has been excellently received, and is "perpetualy imploy'd." There is far more encouragement for modern enterprise in Paris than there is in London; and some of his utterances must have rejoiced the soul of his correspondent. As this, for instance— "The humbug *virtu* is much more out of fashon here than in England, free thinking upon that & other topicks is more common here than amongst you if possible, old pictures & old stories fare's alike, a dark picture is become a damn'd picture." On this account, he inquires anxiously as to the publication of his friend's forthcoming *Analysis*; he has been raising expectations about it, and he wishes to be the first to introduce it into France. From other sources we learn that (perhaps owing to his relations with Belle-Isle, who had been released in

1745) he had been taken up by Marigny, and also by Cochin, then keeper of the King's Drawings, and soon to be Secretary to the Academy, of which Rouquet himself, by express order of Lewis the Fifteenth, was made a member. Finally, as in the case of Cochin, apartments were assigned to him in the Louvre. Whether he ever returned to this country is doubtful; but, as we have seen, the *État des Arts* was printed at Paris in 1755. That it was suggested—or "commanded"—by Mme. de Pompadour's connoisseur brother, to whom it was inscribed, is a not unreasonable supposition.

In any case, M. Rouquet's definition of the "Arts" is a generous one, almost as wide as Marigny's powers, already sufficiently set forth at the outset of this paper. For not only—as in duty bound—does he treat of Architecture, Sculpture, Painting and Engraving, but he also has chapters on Printing, Porcelain, Gold- and Silver-smiths' Work, Jewelry, Music, Declamation, Auctions, Shop-fronts, Cooking, and even on Medicine and Surgery. Oddly enough, he says nothing of one notable art with which Marigny was especially identified, that "art of creating landscape"—as Walpole happily calls Gardening—which, in this not very "shining period," entered upon a fresh development under Bridgeman and William Kent. Although primarily a Londoner,

E

one would think that M. Rouquet must certainly have had some experience, if not of the efforts of the innovators, at least of the very Batavian preformances of Messrs. London and Wise of Brompton; or that he should have found at Nonsuch or Theobalds—at Moor Park or Hampton Court —the pretext for some of his pages—if only to ridicule those "verdant sculptures" at which Pope, who played no small part in the new movement, had laughed in the *Guardian*; or those fantastic "coats of arms and mottoes in yew, box and holly" over which Walpole also made merry long after in the famous essay so neatly done into French by his friend the Duc de Nivernais. M. Rouquet's curious reticence in this matter cannot have been owing to any consideration for Hogarth's old enemy, William Kent, for Kent had been dead seven years when the *État des Arts* made its appearance.

If, for lack of space, we elect to pass by certain preliminary reflections which the *Monthly Review* rather unkindly dismisses as a "tedious jumble," M. Rouquet's first subject is History Painting, a branch of the art which, under George the Second, attained to no great excellence. For this M. Rouquet gives three main reasons, the first being that afterwards advanced by Hogarth and Reynolds, namely,—the practical exclusion, in Protestant countries, of pictures from churches. A second

cause was the restriction of chamber decorations
to portraits and engravings; and a third, the craze
of the connoisseur for Hogarth's hated "Black
Masters," the productions of defunct foreigners.
And this naturally brings about the following
digression, quite in Hogarth's own way, against
that contemporary charlatan, the picture-dealer:—
"English painters have an obstacle to overcome,
which equally impedes the progress of their talents
and of their fortune. They have to contend with
a class of men whose business it is to sell pictures;
and as, for these persons, traffic in the works of
living, and above all of native artists, would be
impossible, they make a point of decrying them,
and, as far as they can, of confirming amateurs with
whom they have to deal in the ridiculous idea that
the older a picture is the more valuable it becomes.
See, say they (speaking of some modern effort), it
still shines with that ignoble freshness which is to
be found in nature; Time will have to indue it
with his learned smoke—with that sacred cloud
which must some day hide it from the profane eyes
of the vulgar in order to reveal to the initiated
alone the mysterious beauties of a venerable
antiquity."

These words are quite in the spirit of Hogarth's
later "Time smoking a Picture." As a matter of fact,
they are reproduced almost textually from the writer's

letter of five years earlier on the "March to Finchley."
To return, however, to History Painting. According to Rouquet, its leading exponent[1] under George
the Second was Francis Hayman of the "large noses
and shambling legs," now known chiefly as a crony
of Hogarth, and a facile but ineffectual illustrator of
Shakespeare and Cervantes. In 1754, however, his
pictures of *See-Saw, Hot Cockles, Blind Man's Buff,*
and the like, for the supper-boxes at Vauxhall
Gardens, with Sayer's prints therefrom, had made his
name familiar, although he had not yet painted those
more elaborate compositions in the large room next
the Rotunda, over which Fanny Burney's "Holborn
Beau," Mr. Smith, comes to such terrible grief in
ch. xlvi. of *Evelina.* But he had contributed a
"Finding of Moses" to the New Foundling Hospital,
which is still to be seen in the Court Room there,
in company with three other pictures executed concurrently for the remaining compartments, Joseph
Highmore's "Hagar and Ishmael," James Wills's
"Suffer little Children," and Hogarth's "Moses
brought to Pharaoh's Daughter"—the best of the
four, as well as the most successful of Hogarth's
historical pieces. All these, then recently installed,
are mentioned by Rouquet.

[1] This is confirmed by Arthur Murphy: "Every Thing is put out of
Hand by this excellent Artist with the utmost Grace and Delicacy, and his
History-Pieces have, besides their beautiful Colouring, the most lively
Expression of Character" (*Gray's Inn Journal,* February 9, 1754).

It will be observed that he says nothing about
Hogarth's earlier and more ambitious efforts in the
"Grand Style," the "Pool of Bethesda" and the
"Good Samaritan" at St. Bartholomew's, nor of the
"Paul before Felix," also lately added to Lincoln's Inn
Hall—omissions which must have sadly exercised the
"author" of those monumental works when he came
to read his Swiss friend's little treatise. Nor, for the
matter of that, does M. Rouquet, when he treats of
portrait, refer to Hogarth's masterpiece in this kind,
the full-length of Captain Coram at the Foundling.
On the other hand, he says a great deal about
Hogarth which has no very obvious connection with
History Painting. He discusses the *Analysis* and
the serpentine Line of Beauty with far more insight
than many of its author's contemporaries; refers
feelingly to the Act by which in 1735 the painter
had so effectively cornered the pirates; and finally
defines his satirical pictures succinctly as follows:—
"M. Hogarth has given to England a new class of
pictures. They contain a great number of figures,
usually seven or eight inches high. These remarkable performances are, strictly speaking, the history
of certain vices, to a foreign eye often a little over-
charged, but always full of wit and novelty. He
understands in his compositions how to make
pleasant pretext for satirising the ridiculous and
the vicious, by firm and significant strokes, all of

which are prompted by a lively, fertile and judicious imagination."

From History Painting to Portrait in Oil, the title given by M. Rouquet to his next chapter, transition is easy. Some of the artists mentioned above were also portrait painters. Besides Captain Coram, for example, Hogarth had already executed that admirable likeness of himself which is now at Trafalgar Square, and which Rouquet must often have seen in its home at Leicester Fields. Highmore too had certainly at this date painted more than one successful portrait of Samuel Richardson, the novelist; and even Hayman had made essay in this direction with the picture of Lord Orford, now in the National Portrait Gallery. A good many of the painters of the last reign must also, during Rouquet's residence in England, have been alive and active, *e.g.* Jervas, Dahl, Aikman, Thornhill and Richardson. But M. Rouquet devotes most of his pages in this respect to Kneller, whose not altogether beneficent influence long survived him. Strangely enough, Rouquet does not mention that egregious and fashionable face-painter, Sir Joshua's master, Thomas Hudson, whose "fair tied-wigs, blue velvet coats, and white satin waistcoats" (all executed by his assistants) reigned undisputed until he was eclipsed by his greater pupil. The two artists in portraiture selected by Rouquet for special notice are Allan

Ramsay and the younger Vanloo (Jean Baptiste).
Both were no doubt far above their predecessors;
but Ramsay would specially appeal to Rouquet by
his continental training, and Vanloo by his French
manner and the superior variety of his attitudes.[1]
The only other name Rouquet recalls is that of
the drapery-painter Joseph Vanhaken; and we
suspect it is to Rouquet that we owe the pleasant
anecdote of the two painters who, for the sum of
£800 a year, pre-empted his exclusive and inestimable
services, to the wholesale discomfiture of their brethren
of the brush. The rest shall be told in Rouquet's
words:—"The best [artists] were no longer able to
paint a hand, a coat, a background; they were forced
to learn, which meant additional labour—what a
misfortune! Henceforth there arrived no more to
Vanhaken from different quarters of London, nor by
coach from the most remote towns of England,
canvases of all sizes, where one or more heads were
painted, under which the painter who forwarded
them had been careful to add, pleasantly enough, the

[1] Another French writer, the Abbé le Blanc, gives a depressing account
of English portraits before Vanloo came to England: "At some distance
one might easily mistake a dozen of them for twelve copies of the same
original. Some have the head turned to the left, others to the right; and
this is the most sensible difference to be observed between them. Moreover, excepting the face, you find in all the same neck, the same arms,
the same flesh, the same attitude; and to say all, you observe no more life
than design in those pretended portraits. Properly speaking, they [the
artists] are not painters, they know how to lay colours on the canvas; but
they know not how to animate it" (*Letters on the English and French
Nations*, 1747, i. 160).

description of the figures, stout or slim, great or small, which were to be appended. Nothing could be more absurd than this arrangement; but it would exist still—if Vanhaken existed."[1]

La peinture à l'huile, C'est bien difficile; *Mais c'est beaucoup plus beau Que la peinture à l'eau.*" About *la peinture à l'eau,* M. Rouquet says very little, in all probability because the English Water Colour School, which, with the advance of topographic art, grew so rapidly in the second half of the century, was yet to come. He refers, however, with approval to the *gouaches* of Joseph Goupy, Lady Burlington's drawing-master, perhaps better known to posterity by his (or her ladyship's) caricature of Handel as the "Charming Brute." (Caricature, by the way, is a branch of Georgian Art which M. Rouquet neglects.) As regards landscape and animal painting, he "abides in generalities"; but he must have been acquainted with the sea pieces of Monamy, and Hogarth's and Walpole's friend Samuel Scott; and should, one would think, have known of the horses and dogs of Wootton and Seymour. Upon Enamel he might be expected to enlarge, although he mentions but one master, his own model, Zincke, who carried the art of portrait in this way much farther than any predecessor. Moreover, like Petitot, he made discoveries which he was wise enough to keep to himself.

---

[1] He died in 1749.

"It is most humiliating," says Rouquet, "for the genius of painting that it can sometimes exist alone. M. Zincke left no pupil." Seeing that Rouquet is also accused of jealously guarding his own contributions to the perfection of his art, the words are—as Diderot says—remarkable.

With Sculpture, chiefly employed at this date for mortuary purposes, he has less opportunity of being indefinite, since there were but three notabilities, Scheemakers, Rysbraek, and Roubillac,—all foreigners. Of these Scheemakers, whom Chesterfield regarded as a mere stone-cutter, and who did the Shakespeare in Westminster Abbey, is certainly the least considerable. Next comes Rysbraek, whom Walpole and Rouquet would put highest, the latter apparently because Rysbraek had been spoken of contemptuously by the Abbé le Blanc. But the first is assuredly Roubillac, whose monument to Mrs. Nightingale, however, belongs to a later date than the *État des Arts,* though he had already achieved the masterly figure of Eloquence on the Argyll monument. The only other sculptor referred to by Rouquet is Gabriel Cibber, whose statues of Madness and Melancholy, long at Bedlam, and now at South Kensington, certainly deserve his praise. But Cibber died in 1700, and belongs to the Caroline epoch. He no doubt owes his place in the *État des Arts* to the fact that he had been abused in the already-mentioned *Letters on the English and French Nations*.

At this point we may turn M. Rouquet's pages more rapidly. It is not necessary to linger over his account of Silk Stuffs, more excellent in his opinion by their material than their make up. Under Medallists he commends the clever medals of great men by his compatriot, Anthony Dassier; under Printing he refers to that liberty of the Press which, in England, amounted to impunity. "A few too thinly disguised blasphemies; a few too rash reflections upon the Government, a few defamatory libels —are the sole things which, at the present time, are not allowed." And this brings about the following lively and very accurate description of the eighteenth-century newspaper:—"One of the most notable peculiarities which liberty of the Press produces in England, is the swarm of fugitive sheets and half-sheets which one sees break forth every morning, except Sunday, covering all the coffee-house tables. Twenty of these different papers, under different titles, appear each day; some contain a moral or philosophical discourse; the majority of the rest offer political, and frequently seditious, comments on some party question. In them is to be found the news of Europe, England, London, and the day before. Their authors profess to be familiar with the most secret deliberations of the Cabinet, which they make public. If a fire occurs in a chimney or elsewhere; if a theft or a murder has taken place; if any one commits suicide from *ennui* or despair, the public is informed thereof on the morning after with the utmost amount of detail. After these articles come advertisements of all sorts, and in very great numbers. In addition to those of different things which it is desired to let, sell or purchase, there are some that are amusing. If a man's wife runs away he declares that he will not be liable for any debts she may contract; and as a matter of fact, this precaution, according to the custom of the country, is essential if he desires to secure himself from doing so. He threatens with all the rigour of the law those who dare to give his wife an asylum. Another publishes the particulars of his fortune, his age and his position, and adds that he is prepared to unite himself to any woman whose circumstances are such as he requires and describes; he further gives the address where communications must be sent for the negotiation and conclusion of the business. There are other notices which describe a woman who has been seen at the play or elsewhere, and announces that some one has determined to marry her. If any one has a dream which seems to him to predict that a certain number will be lucky in the lottery, he proclaims that fact, and offers a consideration to the possessor of the number if he cares to dispose of it."

After these come the advertisements of the Quack

Doctors. Of the account of belles-lettres in 1754, two years after *Amelia* and in the actual year of *Sir Charles Grandison,* M. Rouquet's report is not flattering:—"The presses of England, made celebrated by so many masterpieces of wit and science, now scarcely print anything but miserable and insipid romances, repulsive volumes, frigid and tedious letters, where the most tasteless puerility passes for wit and genius, and an inflamed imagination exerts itself under the pretext of forming manners." It is possible that the last lines are aimed at Richardson; certainly they describe the post-Richardsonian novel. But that the passage does not in any part refer to Fielding is clear from the fact that the writer presently praises *Joseph Andrews,* coupling it with *Gil Blas.*

Mezzotint, Gem-cutting, Chasing (which serves to bring in M. Rouquet's countryman, Moser), Jewelry, China, (*i.e.* Chelsea ware) are all successfully treated with more or less minuteness, while, under Architecture, are described the eighteenth-century house, and the new bridge at Westminster of another Swiss, Labelye, who is not named. "The architect is a foreigner," says Rouquet, who considered he had been inadequately rewarded. "It must be confessed (he adds drily) that in England this is a life-long disqualification." From Architecture the writer passes to the oratory of the Senate, the Pulpit and the Stage. In the last case exception is made for

"*le célébre M. Garic*," whose only teacher is declared
to be Nature. As regards the rest, M. Rouquet thus
describes the prevailing style:—"The declamation of
the English stage is turgid, full of affectation, and
perpetually pompous. Among other peculiarities, it
frequently admits a sort of dolorous exclamation,—
a certain long-drawn tone of voice, so woeful and so
lugubrious that it is impossible not to be depressed
by it." This reads like a recollection of Quin in the
Horatio of Rowe's *Fair Penitent*.

Upon Cookery M. Rouquet is edifying; and concerning the eighteenth-century physician, with his tye-
wig and gilt-head cane, sprightly and not unmalicious.
But we must now confine ourselves to quoting a
few detached passages from this discursive chronicle.
The description of Ranelagh (in the chapter on Music)
is too lengthy to reproduce. Here is that of the
older Vauxhall:—"The Vauxhall concert takes place
in a garden singularly decorated. The Director of
Amusements in this garden [Jonathan Tyers] gains
and spends successively considerable annual sums.
He was born for such enterprises. At once spirited
and tasteful, he shrinks from no expense where the
amusement of the public is concerned, and the public,
in its turn, repays him liberally. Every year he adds
some fresh decoration, some new and exceptional
scene. Sculpture, Painting, Music, bestir themselves
periodically to render this resort more agreeable by

the variety of their different productions: in this way opportunities of relaxation are infinite in England, above all at London; and thus Music plays a prominent part. The English take their pleasure without amusing themselves, or amuse themselves without enjoyment, except at table, and there only up to the point when sleep supervenes to the fumes of wine and tobacco."

Elsewhere M. Rouquet, like M. le Blanc before him, is loud in his denunciation of the pitiful practices of Vails-giving, which blocks the vestibule of every English house with an army of servants "ranged in line, according to their rank," and ready "to receive, or rather exact, the contribution of every guest." The excellent Jonas Hanway wrote a pamphlet reprehending this objectionable custom. Hogarth steadily set his face against it; but Reynolds is reported to have given his man £100 a year for the door. Here, from another place, is a description of one of those popular auctions, at which, in the *Marriage À-la-Mode,* my Lady Squanderfield purchases the *bric-à-brac* of Sir Timothy Babyhouse. The scene is probably Cock's in the Piazza at Covent Garden:—"Nothing is so diverting as this kind of sale—the number of those assembled, the diverse passions which animate them, the pictures, the auctioneer himself, his very rostrum, all contribute to the variety of the spectacle. There you see the faithless broker purchasing in secret what he openly depreciates; or—to spread a dangerous snare—pretending to secure with avidity a picture which already belongs to him. There, some are tempted to buy; and some repent of having bought. There, out of pique and bravado, another shall pay fifty louis for an article which he would not have thought worth five and twenty, had he not been ashamed to draw back when the eyes of a crowded company were upon him. There, you may see a woman of condition turn pale at the mere thought of losing a paltry pagoda which she does not want, and, in any other circumstances, would never have desired."

A closing word as to M. Rouquet himself. The *État des Arts* was duly noticed by the critics—contemptuously by the *Monthly Review,* and sympathetically by the *Gentleman's* and the *Scots Magazine.* In 1755, the year to which it belongs, its author put forth another work—*L'Art Nouveau de la Peinture en Fromage ou en Ramequin* [toasted cheese], *inventé pour suivre le louable projet de trouver graduellement des façons de peindre inférieures à celles qui existent.* This, as its title imports, is a skit, levelled at the recent *Histoire et Secret de la Peinture en Cire* of Diderot, who nevertheless refers to Rouquet under *Émail,* in the *Dictionnaire Encyclopédique,* as "*un homme habile.*" He seems, however (like "*la*

peinture à l'huile)", to have been somewhat
"*difficile*"; and as we have said, his discoveries
(for he had that useful element in enamel-work,
considerable chemical knowledge), like Zincke's,
perished with him. Several of his portraits, notably
those of Cochin and Marigny, were exhibited at the
Paris Salons. Whether he was overparted, or overworked, in the Pompadour atmosphere; or whether
he succumbed to the "continual headache" of which
he speaks in his letter to Hogarth, his health gradually
declined. In the last year of his life, his reason gave
way; and when he died in 1759, it was as an inmate
of Charenton.

THE FRIEND OF HUMANITY AND
THE RHYMER

THE FRIEND OF HUMANITY AND THE RHYMER

"Emam tua carmina sanus?"—MARTIAL

F. OF H. I WANT a verse. It gives you little pains;—
You just sit down, and draw upon your
brains.
Come, now, be amiable.

R.   To hear you talk,
You'd make it easier to fly than walk.
You seem to think that rhyming is a thing
You can produce if you but touch a
spring;
That fancy, fervour, passion—and what
not,
Are just a case of "penny in the slot."
You should reflect that no evasive bird
Is half so shy as is your fittest word;
And even similes, however wrought,
Like hares, before you cook them, must be
caught;—
Impromptus, too, require elaboration,

And (unlike eggs) grow fresh by incuba-
tion;
Then,—as to epigrams . . .

F. of H.   Nay, nay, I've done.
I did but make petition.   You make fun.

R.   Stay.   I am grave.   Forgive me if I
              ramble:
              But, then, a negative needs some preamble
              To break the blow.   I feel with you, in
                  truth,
              These complex miseries of Age and Youth;
              I feel with you—and none can feel it more
              Than I—this burning Problem of the
                  Poor;
              The Want that grinds, the Mystery of Pain,
              The Hearts that sink, and never rise
                  again;—
              How shall I set this to some careless screed,
              Or jigging stave, when Help is what you
                  need,
              Help, Help,—more Help?

F. of H.   I fancied that with ease
              You'd scribble off some verses that might
                  please,
              And so give help to us.

R.   Why then—TAKE THESE!

THE PARENT'S ASSISTANT

THE PARENT'S ASSISTANT

ONE of the things that perplexes the dreamer—for in spite of the realists, there are dreamers still—is the almost complete extinction of the early editions of certain popular works. The pompous, respectable, full-wigged folios, with their long lists of subscribers, and their magniloquent dedications, find their permanent abiding-places in noblemen's collections, where, unless—with the *Chrysostom* in Pope's verses—they are used for the smoothing of bands or the pressing of flowers, no one ever disturbs their drowsy diuturnity. Their bulk makes them sacred: like the regimental big drum, they are too large to be mislaid. But where are all the first copies of that little octavo of 246 pages, price eighteenpence, "Printed by T. Maxey for Rich. Marriot, in S. Dunstans Church-yard, Fleetstreet" in 1653, which constitutes the *editio princeps* of Walton's *Angler*? Probably they were worn out in the pockets of Honest Izaak's "brothers of the Angle," or left to bake and cockle in the sunny corners of wasp-haunted alehouse windows, or dropped in the deep grass by some casual owner, more careful for flies and caddis-worms, or possibly for the contents of a leathern bottle, than all the "choicely-good" madrigals of Maudlin the milkmaid. In any case, there are very few of the little tomes, with their quaint "coppers" of fishes, in existence now, nor is it silver that pays for them. And that other eighteenpenny book, put forth by *"Nath. Ponder* at the *Peacock* in the *Poultrey* near *Cornhil"* five and twenty years later,—*The Pilgrim's Progress from This World, to That which is to come,*—why is it that there are only five known copies, none quite perfect, now extant, of which the best sold not long since for more than £1400? Of these five, the first that came to light had been preserved owing to its having taken sanctuary, almost upon publication, in a great library, where it was forgotten. But the others that passed over Mr. Ponder's counter in the Poultry,—were they all lost, thumbed and dog's-eared out of being? They are gone,—that is all you can say; and gone apparently beyond reach of recovery.

These remarks,—which scarcely rise to the dignity of reflections—have been suggested by the difficulty which the writer has experienced in obtaining particulars as to the earliest form of *The Parent's Assistant*. As a matter of course, children's books are more liable to disappear than any others. They are sooner torn, soiled, dismembered, disintegrated—

sooner find their way to that mysterious unlocated
limbo of lost things, which engulfs so much. Yet
one scarcely expected that even the British Museum
would not have possessed a copy of the first issue of
Miss Edgeworth's book. Such, however, seems to
be the case. According to the catalogue, there is
nothing earlier at Bloomsbury than a portion of the
second edition; and from the inexplicit and conjectural
manner in which most of the author's biographers
speak of the work, it can scarcely—outside private
collections—be very easily accessible. Fortunately
the old *Monthly Review* for September, 1796, with
most exemplary forethought for posterity, gives, as a
heading to its notice, a precise and very categorical
account of the first impression. *The Parent's Assistant; or, Stories for Children* was, it appears, published
in two parts, making three small duodecimo volumes.
The price, bound, was six shillings. There was no
author's name; but it was said to be "by E. M." (*i.e.*
Edgeworth, Maria), and the publisher was Cowper's
Dissenter publisher, Joseph Johnson of No. 72, St.
Paul's Churchyard. Part I. contained "The Little
Dog Trusty; or, The Liar and the Boy of Truth";
"The Orange Man; or, the Honest Boy and the
Thief"; "Lazy Lawrence"; "Tarleton"; and "The
False Key"; Part II., "The Purple Jar," "The
Bracelets," "Mademoiselle Panache," "The Birthday
Present," "Old Poz," and "The Mimic." In the

same year, 1796, a second edition apeared, apparently with some supplementary stories, *e.g.*: "Barring Out," and in 1800 came a third edition in six volumes. In this the text was increased by "Simple Susan," "The Little Merchants," "The Basket Woman," "The White Pigeon," "The Orphans," "Waste Not, Want Not," "Forgive and Forget," and "Eton Montem." One story, "The Purple Jar" at the beginning of Part II. of the first edition, was withdrawn, and afterwards included in another series, while the stories entitled respectively "Little Dog Trusty" and "The Orange Man" have disappeared from the collection, probably for the reason given in one of the first prefaces, namely, that they "were written for a much earlier age than any of the others, and with such a perfect simplicity of expression as, to many, may appear insipid and ridiculous." The six volumes of the third edition came out successively on the first day of the first six months of 1800. The Monthly Reviewer of the first edition, it may be added, was highly laudatory; and his commendations show that the early critics of the author were fully alive to her distinctive qualities. "The moral and prudential lessons of these volumes," says the writer, "are judiciously chosen; and the stories are invented with great ingenuity, and are happily contrived to excite curiosity and awaken feeling without the aid of improbable fiction or extravagant adventure. The language is varied in its degree of simplicity, to suit the pieces to different ages, but is throughout neat and correct; and, without the least approach towards vulgarity or meanness, it is adapted with peculiar felicity to the understandings of children. The author's taste, in this class of writing, appears to have been formed on the best models; and the work will not discredit a place on the same shelf with Berquin's *Child's Friend,* Mrs. Barbauld's *Lessons for Children,* and Dr. Aikin's *Evenings at Home.* The story of 'Lazy Lawrence' " —the notice goes on—"is one of the best lectures on industry which we have ever read." The *Critical Review,* which also gave a short account of the *Parent's Assistant* in its number for January 1797, does not rehearse the contents. But it confirms the title, etc., adding that the price, in boards, was 4s. 6d.; and its praise, though brief, is very much to the point. "The present production is particularly sensible and judicious; the stories are well written, simple, and affecting; calculated, not only for moral improvement, but to exercise the best affections of the human heart."

With one of the books mentioned by the *Monthly Review—Evenings at Home*—Miss Edgeworth was fully prepared, at all events as regards format, to associate herself. "The stories," she says in a letter to her cousin, Miss Sophy Ruxton, "are printed and bound the same size as *Evenings at Home,* and I am afraid you will dislike the title." Her father had sent the book to press as the *Parent's Friend,* a name no doubt suggested by the *Ami des Enfants* of Berquin; but "Mr. Johnson [the publisher]," continues Miss Edgeworth, "has degraded it into *The Parent's Assistant,* which I dislike particularly, from association with an old book of arithmetic called *The Tutor's Assistant.*" The ground of objection is not very formidable; but the *Parent's Assistant* is certainly an infelicitous name. From some other of the author's letters we are able to trace the gradual growth of the work. Mr. Edgeworth, her father, an utilitarian of much restless energy, and many projects, was greatly interested in education,—or, as he would have termed it, *practical* education,—and long before this date, as early, indeed, as May 1780, he had desired his daughter, while she was still a girl at a London school, to write him a tale about the length of a *Spectator,* upon the topic of "Generosity," to be taken from history or romance. This was her first essay in fiction; and it was pronounced by the judge to whom it was submitted,—in competition with a rival production by a young gentleman from Oxford,—to be an excellent story, and extremely well-written, although with this commendation was coupled the somewhat damaging inquiry,—"But where's the Generosity?" The question cannot be answered now, as the manuscript has not been preserved, though the inconvenient query, we are told, became a kind of personal proverb with the young author, who was wont to add that this first effort contained "a sentence of inextricable confusion between a saddle, a man, and his horse." This was a defect from which she must have speedily freed herself, since her style, as her first reviewer allowed, is conspicuously direct and clear. Accuracy in speaking and writing had, indeed, been early impressed upon her. Her father's doctrinaire ally and co-disciplinarian, Mr. Thomas Day, later the author of *Sandford and Merton,* and apparently the first person of whom it is affirmed that "he talked like a book," had been indefatigable in bringing this home to his young friend, when she visited him in her London school-days. Not content alone to dose her copiously with Bishop Berkeley's Tar Water—the chosen beverage of Young and Richardson—he was unwearied in ministering to her understanding. "His severe reasoning and uncompromising love of truth awakened her powers, and the questions he put to her, the necessity of perfect accuracy in her answers, suited the bent of her mind. Though such strictness was not always agreeable, she even then perceived its advantages, and in after life was deeply grateful to Mr. Day."[1]

The training she underwent from the inexorable

---

[1] *Maria Edgeworth,* by Helen Zimmern, 1888, p. 13.

Mr. Day was continued by her father when she quitted school, and moved with her family to the parental seat at Edgeworthstown in Ireland. Mr. Edgeworth, whose principles were as rigorous as those of his friend, devoted himself early to initiating her into business habits. He taught her to copy letters, to keep accounts, to receive rents, and, in short, to act as his agent and factotum. She frequently accompanied him in the many disputes and difficulties which arose with his Irish tenantry; and apart from the insight which this must have afforded her into the character and idiosyncrasies of the people, she no doubt very early acquired that exact knowledge of leases and legacies and dishonest factors which is a noticeable feature even of her children's books.[1] It is some time, however, before we hear of any successor to "Generosity"; but, in 1782, her father, with a view to provide her with an occupation for her leisure, proposed to her to prepare a translation of the *Adèle et Théodore* of Madame de Genlis, those letters upon education by which that gentle and multifarious moralist acquired—to use her own words—at once "the suffrages of the public, and the irreconcilable hatred of all the so-called philosophers and their partisans." At first there had been no definite thought of print in Mr. Edgeworth's mind. But as the work

[1] Cf. "Attorney Case" in the story of "Simple Susan."

progressed, the idea gathered strength; and he began to prepare his daughter's manuscript for the press. Then, unhappily, when the first volume was finished, Holcroft's complete translation appeared, and made the labour needless. Yet it was not without profit. It had been excellent practice in aiding Miss Edgeworth's faculty of expression, and increasing her vocabulary—to say nothing of the influence which the portraiture of individuals and the satire of reigning follies which are the secondary characteristics of Madame de Genlis's most well-known work, may have had on her own subsequent efforts as a novelist. Meanwhile her mentor, Mr. Day, was delighted at the interruption of her task. He possessed, to the full, that rooted antipathy to feminine authorship of which we find so many traces in Miss Burney's novels and elsewhere; and he wrote to congratulate Mr. Edgeworth on having escaped the disgrace of having a translating daughter. At this time, as already stated, he himself had not become the author of *Sandford and Merton,* which, as a matter of fact, owed its inception to the Edgeworths, being at first simply intended as a short story to be inserted in the *Harry and Lucy* Mr. Edgeworth wrote in conjunction with his second wife, Honora Sneyd. As regards the question of publication, both Maria and her father, although sensible of Mr. Day's prejudices, appear to have deferred to his arguments. Nor were these even lost to the public, for we are informed that, in Miss Edgeworth's first book, ten years later, the *Letters to Literary Ladies,* she employed and embodied much that he had advanced. But for the present, she continued to write—though solely for her private amusement—essays, little stories, and dramatic sketches. One of these last must have been "Old Poz," a pleasant study of a country justice and a *gazza ladra,* which appeared in Par⁺ II. of the first issue of the *Parent's Assistant,* and which, we are told, was acted by the Edgeworth children in a little theatre erected in the dining-room for the purpose. According to her sisters, it was Miss Edgeworth's practice first to write her stories on a slate, and then to read them out. If they were approved, she transcribed them fairly. "Her writing for children" —says one of her biographers—"was a natural outgrowth of a practical study of their wants and fancies; and her constant care of the younger children gave her exactly the opportunity required to observe the development of mind incident to the age and capacity of several little brothers and sisters." According to her own account, her first critic was her father. "Whenever I thought of writing anything, I always told him [my father] my first rough plans; and always, with the instinct of a good critic, he used to fix immediately upon that which would best answer the purpose.—*'Sketch that, and shew it to me.'*—These words, from the experience of his sagacity, never failed to inspire me with hope of success. It was then sketched. Sometimes, when I was fond of a particular part, I used to dilate on it in the sketch; but to this he always objected—'I don't want any of your painting—none of your drapery!—I can imagine all that—let me see the bare skeleton.' "

Of the first issue of the *Parent's Assistant* in 1796, a sufficient account has already been given. In the "Preface" the practical intention of several of the stories is explicitly set forth. "Lazy Lawrence," we are told, illustrates the advantages of industry, and demonstrates that people feel cheerful and happy whilst they are employed; while "Tarleton" represents "the danger and the folly of that weakness of mind, and that easiness to be led, which too often pass for good nature"; "The False Key" points out some of the evils to which a well-educated boy, on first going to service, is exposed from the profligacy of his fellow-servants; "The Mimic," the drawback of vulgar acquaintances; "Barring Out," the errors to which a high spirit and the love of party are apt to lead, and so forth. In the final paragraph stress is laid upon what every fresh reader must at once recognise as the supreme merit of the stories, namely, their dramatic faculty, or (in the actual words of the "Preface"), their art of "keeping alive hope and fear and curiosity, by some degree of intricacy."[1] The plausibility of invention, the amount of ingenious contrivance and of clever expedient in these professedly nursery stories, is indeed extraordinary; and nothing can exceed the dexterity with which—to use Dr. Johnson's words concerning *She Stoops to Conquer*—"the incidents are so prepared as not to seem improbable." There is no better example of this than the admirable tale of "The Mimic," in which the most unlooked-for occurrences succeed each other in the most natural way, while the disappearance at the end of the little sweep, who has levanted up the chimney in Frederick's new blue coat and buff waistcoat, is a master-stroke. Everybody has forgotten everything about him until the precise moment when he is needed to supply the fitting surprise of the finish, —a surprise which is only to be compared to that other revelation in *The Rose and the Ring* of Thackeray, where the long-lost and obnoxious porter at Valoroso's palace, having been turned by the Fairy Blackstick into a door knocker for his insolence, is restored to the sorrowing Servants' Hall exactly when his services are again required in the capacity of Mrs. Gruffanuff's husband. But in Miss Edge-

---

[1] The "Preface to Parents"—Miss Emily Lawless suggests to me—was probably by Mr. Edgeworth.

worth's little fable there is no fairy agency. "Fairies were not much in her line," says Lady Ritchie, Thackeray's daughter, "but philanthropic manufacturers, liberal noblemen, and benevolent ladies in travelling carriages, do as well and appear in the nick of time to distribute rewards or to point a moral."

Although, by their sub-title, these stories are avowedly composed for children, they are almost as attractive to grown-up readers. This is partly owing to their narrative skill, partly also to the clear characterisation, which already betrays the coming author of *Castle Rackrent* and *Belinda* and *Patronage*—the last, under its first name of *The Freeman Family,* being already partly written, although many years were still to pass before it saw the light in 1814. Readers, wise after the event, might fairly claim to have foreseen from some of the personages in the *Parent's Assistant* that the author, however sedulous to describe "such situations only . . as children can easily imagine," was not able entirely to resist tempting specimens of human nature like the bibulous Mr. Corkscrew, the burglar butler in "The False Key," or Mrs. Pomfret, the housekeeper of the same story, whose prejudices against the *Villaintropic* Society, and its unholy dealing with the "*drugs* and *refuges*" of humanity, are quite in the style of the Mrs. Slipslop of a great artist whose works one would

scarcely have expected to encounter among the
paper-backed and grey-boarded volumes which lined
the shelves at Edgeworthstown. Mrs. Theresa
Tattle, again, in "The Mimic," is a type which
requires but little to fit it for a subordinate part in
a novel, as is also Lady Diana Sweepstakes in "Waste
not, Want not." In more than one case, we seem
to detect an actual portrait. Mr. Somerville of
Somerville ("The White Pigeon"), to whom that
"little town" belonged,—who had done so much
"to inspire his tenantry with a taste for order and
domestic happiness, and took every means in his
power to encourage industrious, well-behaved people
to settle in his neighbourhood,"—can certainly be
none other than the father of the writer of the
Parent's Assistant, the busy and beneficent, but
surely eccentric, Mr. Edgeworth of Edgeworthstown.

When, in 1849, the first two volumes of
Macaulay's *History* were issued, Miss Edgeworth,
then in her eighty-third winter, was greatly delighted
to find her name, coupled with a compliment to one
of her characters, enshrined in a note to chap. vi.
But her gratification was qualified by the fact that
she could discover no similar reference to her friend,
Sir Walter Scott. The generous "twinge of pain,"
to which she confesses, was intelligible. Scott had
always admired her genius, and she admired his. In
the "General Preface" to the *Waverley Novels,*

twenty years before, he had gone so far as to say that, without hoping to emulate "the rich humour, pathetic tenderness, and admirable tact" of Miss Edgeworth, he had attempted to do for his own country what she had done for hers; and it is clear, from other sources, that this was no mere form of words.   And he never wavered in his admiration. In his last years, not many months before his death, when he had almost forgotten her name, he was still talking kindly of her work.   Speaking to Mrs. John Davy of Miss Austen and Miss Ferrier, he said: "And there's that Irish lady, too—but I forget everybody's name now" . . . "she's *very* clever, and best in the little touches too.   I'm sure in that children's story, where the little girl parts with her lamb, and the little boy brings it back to her again, there's nothing for it but just to put down the book and cry."[1]   The reference is to "Simple Susan," the longest and prettiest tale in the *Parent's Assistant*.

Another anecdote pleasantly connects the same book with a popular work of a later writer. Readers of *Cranford* will recall the feud between the Johnson-loving Miss Jenkyns of that story and its *Pickwick*-loving Captain Brown.   The Captain—as is well-known—met his death by a railway accident, just after he had been studying the last monthly

---

[1] Lockhart's *Life of Sir Walter Scott,* ch. lxxxi. *ad finem.*

"green covers" of Dickens. Years later, the assumed narrator of *Cranford* visits Miss Jenkyns, then falling into senility. She still vaunts *The Rambler*; still maunders vaguely of the "strange old book, with the queer name, poor Captain Brown was killed for reading—that book by Mr. Boz, you know—*Old Poz*; when I was a girl—but that's a long time ago—I acted Lucy in *Old Poz*." There can be no mistake. Lucy is the justice's daughter in Miss Edgeworth's little chamber-drama.

A PLEASANT INVECTIVE AGAINST PRINTING

A PLEASANT INVECTIVE AGAINST PRINTING

"Flee fro the PREES, and dwelle with sothfastnesse."—
CHAUCER, *Balade de Bon Conseil*

THE Press is too much with us, small and great:
We are undone of chatter and *on dit,*
Report, retort, rejoinder, repartee,
Mole-hill and mare's nest, fiction up-to-date,
Babble of booklets, bicker of debate,
Aspect of A., and attitude of B.—
A waste of words that drive us like a sea,
Mere derelict of Ourselves, and helpless freight!

"O for a lodge in some vast wilderness!"
Some region unapproachable of Print,
Where never cablegram could gain access,
And telephones were not, nor any hint
Of tidings new or old, but Man might pipe
His soul to Nature,—careless of the Type!

TWO MODERN BOOK ILLUSTRATORS

GROUP OF CHILDREN, FOR "THE LIBRARY."

(From the original pen-drawing.)

TWO MODERN BOOK ILLUSTRATORS

I. KATE GREENAWAY

IN the world of pictorial recollection there are many territories, the natives of which you may recognise by their characteristics as surely as Ophelia recognises her true-love by his cockle-hat and sandal shoon. There is the land of grave gestures and courteous inclinations, of dignified leave-takings and decorous greetings; where the ladies (like Richardson's Pamela) don the most charming round-eared caps and frilled *négligés*; where the gentlemen sport ruffles and bag-wigs and spotless silk stockings, and invariably exhibit shapely calves above their silver shoe-buckles; where you may come in St. James's Park upon a portly personage with a star, taking an alfresco pinch of snuff after that leisurely style in which a pinch of snuff should be taken, so as not to endanger a lace cravat or a canary-coloured vest; where you may seat yourself on a bench by Rosamond's Pond in company with a tremulous mask who is evidently expecting the arrival of a "pretty fellow"; or happen suddenly, in a secluded side-walk, upon a damsel in muslin and a dark hat, who is hurriedly scrawling a *poulet,* not without obvious signs of perturbation. But whatever the denizens of this country are doing, they are always elegant and always graceful, always appropriately grouped against their fitting background of high-ceiled rooms and striped hangings, or among the urns and fish-tanks of their sombre-shrubbed gardens. This is the land of STOTHARD.

In the adjoining country there is a larger sense of colour—a fuller pulse of life. This is the region of delightful dogs and horses and domestic animals of all sorts; of crimson-faced hosts and buxom ale-wives; of the most winsome and black-eyed milkmaids and the most devoted lovers and their lasses; of the most headlong and horn-blowing huntsmen—a land where Madam Blaize forgathers with the impeccable worthy who caused the death of the Mad Dog; where John Gilpin takes the Babes in the Wood *en croupe*; and the bewitchingest Queen of Hearts coquets the Great Panjandrum himself "with the little round button at top"—a land, in short, of the most kindly and light-hearted fancies, of the freshest and breeziest and healthiest types—which is the land of CALDECOTT.

Finally, there is a third country, a country inhabited almost exclusively by the sweetest little child-figures that have ever been invented, in the quaintest and prettiest costumes, always happy, always gravely playful,—and nearly always playing; always set in the most attractive framework of flower-knots, or blossoming orchards, or red-roofed cottages with dormer windows. Everywhere there are green fields, and daisies, and daffodils, and pearly skies of spring, in which a kite is often flying. No children are quite like the dwellers in this land; they are so gentle, so unaffected in their affectation, so easily pleased, so trustful and so confiding. And this is GREENAWAY-land.

It is sixty years since Thomas Stothard died, and only fifteen since Randolph Caldecott closed his too brief career.[1] And now Kate Greenaway, who loved the art of both, and in her own gentle way possessed something of the qualities of each, has herself passed away. It will rest with other pens to record her personal characteristics, and to relate the story of her life. I who write this was privileged to know her a little, and to receive from her frequent presents of her books; but I should shrink from anything approaching a description of the quiet, unpretentious, almost homely little lady, whom it was always a pleasure to meet and to talk with. If I here permit myself to recall one or two incidents of our inter-course, it is solely because they bear either upon

[1] This was written in 1902.

her amiable dispositon or her art. I remember that once, during a country walk in Sussex, she gave me a long account of her childhood, which I wish I could repeat in detail. But I know that she told me that she had been brought up in just such a neighbourhood of thatched roofs and "grey old gardens" as she depicts in her drawings; and that in some of the houses, it was her particular and unfailing delight to turn over ancient chests and wardrobes filled with the flowered frocks and capes of the Jane Austen period. As is well known, she corresponded frequently with Ruskin, and possessed numbers of his letters. In his latter years, it had been her practice to write to him periodically—I believe she said once a week. He had long ceased, probably from ill-health, to answer her letters; but she continued to write punctually lest he should miss the little budget of chit-chat to which he had grown accustomed. At another time—in a pleasant country-house which contained many examples of her art—and where she was putting the last touches to a delicately tinted child-angel in the margin of a Bible—I ventured to say, "Why do your children always . . .?" But it is needless to complete the query; the answer alone is important. She looked at me reflectively, and said, after a pause, "Because I see it so."

Answers not dissimilar have been given before by other artists in like case. But it was this rigid

PENCIL-SKETCHES BY MISS GREENAWAY (NO. 1).

fidelity to her individual vision and personal con-
viction which constituted her strength. There are
always stupid, well-meaning busybodies in the world,
who go about making question of the sonneteer why
he does not attempt something epic and homicidal,
or worrying the carver of cherry-stones to try his
hand at a Colossus; but though they disturb and
discompose, they luckily do no material harm. They
did no material harm to Kate Greenaway. She
yielded, no doubt, to pressure put upon her to try
figures on a larger scale; to illustrate books, which
was not her strong point, as it only put fetters upon
her fancy; but, in the main, she courageously preserved the even tenor of her way, which was to
people the artistic demesne she administered with
the tiny figures which no one else could make more
captivating, or clothe more adroitly. It may be
doubted whether the collector will set much store
by Bret Harte's *Queen of the Pirate Isle* or the *Pied
Piper of Hamelin,* suitable at first sight as is the
latter, with its child-element, to her inventive
idiosyncrasy. But he will revel in the dainty scenes
of "Almanacks" (1883 to 1895, and 1897); in the
charming Birthday Book of 1880; in *Mother Goose,
A Day in a Child's Life, Little Ann, Marigold Garden*
and the rest, of which the grace is perennial, though
the popularity for the moment may have waned.

H

I have an idea that *Mother Goose; or, the Old
Nursery Rhymes,* 1881, was one of Miss Greenaway's
favourites, although it may have been displaced in
her own mind by subsequent successes. Nothing
can certainly be more deftly-tinted than the design of
the "old woman who lived under a hill," and peeled
apples; nothing more seductive, in infantile attitude,
than the little boy and girl, who, with their arms
around each other, stand watching the black-cat in
the plum-tree. Then there is Daffy-down-dilly, who
has come up to town, with "a yellow petticoat and a
green gown," in which attire, aided by a straw hat
tied under her chin, she manages to look exceedingly
attractive, as she passes in front of the white house
with the pink roof and the red shutters and the green
palings. One of the most beautiful pictures in this
gallery is the dear little "Ten-o'-clock Scholar" in
his worked smock, as, trailing his blue-and-white
school-bag behind him, he creeps unwillingly to his
lessons at the most picturesque timbered cottage you
can imagine. Another absolutely delightful portrait
is that of "Little Tom Tucker," in sky-blue suit and
frilled collar, singing, with his hands behind him, as
if he never could grow old. And there is not one of
these little compositions that is without its charm of
colour and accessory—blue plates on the dresser in
the background, the parterres of a formal garden
with old-fashioned flowers, quaint dwellings with

PENCIL-SKETCH BY MISS GREENAWAY (NO. 2).

their gates and grass-work, odd corners of country-
side and village street, and all, generally, in the clear
air or sunlight.   For in this favoured Greenaway-
realm, as in the island-valley of Avilion, there

> falls not hail, or rain, or any snow,
> Nor ever wind blows loudly; but it lies
> Deep-meadow'd, happy, fair with orchard-lawns.

To *Mother Goose* followed *A Day in a Child's
Life,* also 1881, and *Little Ann,* 1883.   The former
of these contained various songs set to music by
Mr. Myles B. Foster, the organist of the Foundling
Hospital, and accompanied by designs on rather a
larger scale than those in *Mother Goose.*   It also
included a larger proportion of the floral decorations
which were among the artist's chief gifts.   Foxgloves
and buttercups, tulips and roses, are flung about the
pages of the book; and there are many pictures,
notably one of a little green-coated figure perched
upon a five-barred gate, which repeat the triumphs
of its predecessor.   In *Little Ann and other Poems,*
which is dedicated to the four children of the artist's
friend, the late Frederick Locker Lampson, she
illustrated a selection from the verses for "Infant
Minds" of Jane and Ann Taylor, daughters of that
Isaac Taylor of Ongar, who was first a line engraver
and afterwards an Independent Minister.[1]   The

[1] Since this paper was written, the *Original Poems and Others,* of Ann
and Jane Taylor, with illustrations by F. D. Bedford, and a most interesting
"Introduction" by Mr. E. V. Lucas, have been issued by Messrs. Wells,
Gardner, Darton and Co.

dedication contains a charming row of tiny portraits of the Locker Lampson family. These illustrations may seem to contradict what has been said as to Miss Greenaway's ability to interpret the conceptions of others. But this particular task left her perfectly free to "go her own gait," and to embroider the text which, in this case, was little more than a pretext for her pencil.

In *Marigold Garden,* 1885, Miss Greenaway became her own poet; and next to *Mother Goose,* this is probably her most important effort. The flowers are as entrancing as ever; and the verse makes one wish that the writer had written more. The "Genteel Family" and "Little Phillis" are excellent nursery pieces; and there is almost a Blake-like note about "The Sun Door."

They saw it rise in the morning,
   They saw it set at night,
And they longed to go and see it,
   Ah! if they only might.

The little soft white clouds heard them,
   And stepped from out of the blue;
And each laid a little child softly
   Upon its bosom of dew.

And they carried them higher and higher,
   And they nothing knew any more,
Until they were standing waiting,
   In front of the round gold door.

PENCIL-SKETCHES BY MISS GREENAWAY (NO. 3).

> And they knocked, and called, and entreated
>   Whoever should be within;
> But all to no purpose, for no one
>   Would hearken to let them in.

"*La rime n'est pas riche,*" nor is the technique thoroughly assured; but the thought is poetical. Here is another, "In an Apple-Tree," which reads like a child variation of that haunting "Mimnermus in Church" of the author of *Ionica*:—

> In September, when the apples are red,
> To Belinda I said,
> "Would you like to go away
> To Heaven, or stay
> Here in this orchard full of trees
> All your life?" And she said, "If you please
> I'll stay here—where I know,
> And the flowers grow."

In another vein is the bright little "Child's Song":—

> The King and the Queen were riding
>   Upon a Summer's day,
> And a Blackbird flew above them,
>   To hear what they did say.
>
> The King said he liked apples,
>   The Queen said she liked pears;
> And what shall we do to the Blackbird
>   Who listens unawares?

But, as a rule, it must be admitted of her poetry that, while nearly always poetic in its impulse, it is often halting and inarticulate in its expression.

A few words may be added in regard to the mere facts of Miss Greenaway's career. She was born at 1 Cavendish Street, Hoxton, on the 17th March, 1846, her father being Mr. John Greenaway, a draughtsman on wood, who contributed much to the earlier issues of the *Illustrated London News* and *Punch*. Annual visits to a farm-house at Rolleston in Nottinghamshire—the country residence already referred to—nourished and confirmed her love of nature. Very early she showed a distinct bias towards colour and design of an original kind. She studied at different places, and at South Kensington. Here both she and Lady Butler "would bribe the porter to lock them in when the day's work was done, so that they might labour on for some while more." Her master at Kensington was Richard Burchett, who, forty years ago, was a prominent figure in the art-schools, a well instructed painter, and a teacher exceptionally equipped with all the learning of his craft. Mr. Burchett thought highly of Miss Greenaway's abilities; and she worked under him for several years with exemplary perseverance and industry. She subsequently studied in the Slade School under Professor Legros.

Her first essays in the way of design took the form of Christmas cards, then beginning their now somewhat flagging career, and she exhibited pictures at the Dudley Gallery for some years in succession,

PENCIL-SKETCH BY MISS GREENAWAY (NO. 4).

beginning with 1868. In 1877 she contributed to the Royal Academy a water colour entitled "Musing," and in 1889 was elected a member of the Royal Institute of Painters in Water Colours.

By this date, as will be gathered from what has preceded, Miss Greenaway had made her mark as a producer of children's books, since, in addition to the volumes already specially mentioned, she had issued *Under the Window* (her earliest success), *The Language of Flowers, Kate Greenaway's Painting Book, The Book of Games, King Pepito* and other works. Her last "Almanack," which was published by Messrs. Dent and Co., appeared in 1897. In 1891, the Fine Arts Society exhibited some 150 of her original drawings—an exhibition which was deservedly successful, and was followed by others.[1] As Slade Professor at Oxford, Ruskin, always her fervent admirer, gave her unstinted eulogium; and in France her designs aroused the greatest admiration. The *Débats* had a leading article on her death; and the clever author of *L'Art du Rire,* M. Arsène Alexandre, who had already written appreciatively of her gifts as a *paysagiste,"* and as a *"maîtresse en l'art du sourire, du joli sourire*

---

[1] Among other things these exhibitions revealed the great superiority of the original designs to the reproductions with which the public are familiar —excellent as these are in their way. Probably, if Miss Greenaway's work were now repeated by the latest form of three-colour process, she would be less an "inheritor"—in this respect—"of unfulfilled renown."

d'enfant ingénu et gaiement candide" devoted a column in the *Figaro* to her merits.

It has been noted that, in her later years, Miss Greenaway's popularity was scarcely maintained. It would perhaps be more exact to say that it somewhat fell off with the fickle crowd who follow a reigning fashion, and who unfortunately help to swell the units of a paying community. To the last she gave of her best; but it is the misfortune of distinctive and original work, that, while the public resents versatility in its favourites, it wearies unreasonably of what had pleased it at first—especially if the note be made tedious by imitation. Miss Greenaway's old vogue was in some measure revived by her too-early death on the 6th November, 1901; but, in any case, she is sure of attention from the connoisseur of the future. Those who collect Stothard and Caldecott (and they are many!) cannot afford to neglect either *Marigold Garden* or *Mother Goose*.[1]

---

[1] Since the above article appeared in the *Art Journal,* from which it is here substantially reproduced, Messrs. M. H. Spielmann and G. S. Layard have (1905) devoted a sumptuous and exhaustive volume to Miss Greenaway and her art. To this truly beautiful and sympathetic book I can but refer those of her admirers who are not yet acquainted with it.

A SONG OF THE GREENAWAY CHILD

A SONG OF THE GREENAWAY CHILD

As I went a-walking on *Lavender Hill,*
O, I met a Darling in frock and frill;
And she looked at me shyly, with eyes of blue,
"Are you going a-walking? Then take me too!"

So we strolled to the field where the cowslips grow,
And we played—and we played, for an hour or so;
Then we climbed to the top of the old park wall,
And the Darling she threaded a cowslip ball.

Then we played again, till I said—"My Dear,
This pain in my side, it has grown severe;
I ought to have mentioned I'm past three-score,
And I fear that I scarcely can play any more!"

But the Darling she answered,—"O no! O no!
You must play—you must play.—I sha'n't let you
    go!"
—And I woke with a start and a sigh of despair,
And I found myself safe in my Grandfather's-chair!

TWO MODERN BOOK ILLUSTRATORS

Ernest Brown

his Book

O for a Booke and a shadie Nook,
eyther in-a-doore or out;
With the green leaves whispering
overhede,
Or the streete cryes all about:

Where I mai Reade all at my ease
Both of the Newe and Olde;
For a jollie goode Booke where-
on to looke
Is better to me than Golde

EX LIBRIS

THE BROWN BOOK-PLATE.

(From the original design.)

TWO MODERN BOOK ILLUSTRATORS

II. Mr. Hugh Thomson

In virtue of certain gentle and caressing qualities of style, Douglas Jerrold conferred on one of his contributors—Miss Eliza Meteyard—the pseudonym of "Silverpen." It is in the silver-pensive key that one would wish to write of Mr. Hugh Thomson. There is nothing in his work of elemental strife,—of social problem,—of passion torn to tatters. He leads you by no *terribile via,* —over no "burning Marle." You cannot conceive him as the illustrator of *Paradise Lost,* of Dante's *Inferno*—even of Doré's *Wandering Jew.* But when, after turning over some dozens of his designs, you take stock of your impressions, you discover that your memory is packed with pleasant fancies. You have been among "blown fields" and "flowerful closes"; you have passed quaint roadside-inns and picturesque cottages; you are familiar with the cheery, ever-changing idyll of the highway and the bustle of animal life; with horses that really gallop, and dogs that really bark; with charming male and female figures in the most attractive old-world attire; with happy laughter and artless waggeries; with a hundred intimate details of English domesticity that are pushed just far enough back to lose the hardness of their outline in a softening haze of retrospect. There has been nothing more tragic in your travels than a sprained ankle or an interrupted affair of honour; nothing more blood-curdling than a dream of a dragoon officer knocked out of his saddle by a brickbat. Your flesh has never been made to creep: but the cockles of your heart have been warmed. Mechanically, you raise your hand to lift away your optimistic spectacles. But they are not there. The optimism is in the pictures.

It must be more than a quarter of a century since Mr. Hugh Thomson, arriving from Coleraine in all the ardour of one-and-twenty, invaded the strongholds of English illustration. He came at a fortunate moment. After a few hesitating and tentative attempts upon the newspapers, he obtained an introduction to Mr. Comyns Carr, then engaged in establishing the *English Illustrated Magazine* for Messrs. Macmillan. His recommendation was a scrap-book of minutely elaborated designs for *Vanity Fair*, which he had done (like Reynolds) "out of

SIR ROGER DE COVERLEY AT THE ASSIZES.

(From a first rough pencil-sketch for *Days with Sir Roger de Coverley*.)

pure idleness." Mr. Carr, then, as always, a dis-
criminating critic, with a keen eye to possibilities,
was not slow to detect, among much artistic recollection, something more than uncertain promise; and
although he had already Randolph Caldecott and
Mr. Harry Furniss on his staff, he at once gave
Mr. Thomson a commission for the magazine. The
earliest picture from his hand which appeared was
a fancy representation of the Parade at Bath for a
paper in June, 1884, by the late H. D. Traill; and
he also illustrated (in part) papers on Drawing Room
Dances, on Cricket (by Mr. Andrew Lang), and on
Covent Garden. But graphic and vividly naturalistic
as were his pictures of modern life, his native bias
towards imaginary eighteenth-century subjects (perhaps prompted by boyish studies of Hogarth in the
old Dublin *Penny Magazine*), was already abundantly
manifest. He promptly drifted into what was
eventually to become his first illustrated book, a
series of compositions from the *Spectator*. These
were published in 1886 as a little quarto, entitled
Days with Sir Roger de Coverley.

It was a "temerarious" task to attempt to revive
the types which, from the days of Harrison's *Essay-
ists,* had occupied so many of the earlier illustrators.
But the attempt was fully justified by its success.
One has but to glance at the head-piece to the first
paper, where Sir Roger and "Mr. Spectator" have

alighted from the jolting, springless, heavy-wheeled old coach as the tired horses toil uphill, to recognise at once that here is an artist *en pays de connaissance,* who may fairly be trusted, in the best sense, to "illustrate" his subject. Whatever one's predilections for previous presentments, it is impossible to resist Sir Roger (young, slim, and handsome), carving the perverse widow's name upon a tree-trunk; or Sir Roger at bowls, or riding to hounds, or listening—with grave courtesy—to Will Wimble's long-winded and circumstantial account of the taking of the historic jack. Nor is the conception less happy of that amorous fine-gentleman ancestor of the Coverleys who first made love by squeezing the hand; or of that other Knight of the Shire who so narrowly escaped being killed in the Civil Wars because he was sent out of the field upon a private message, the day before Cromwell's "crowning mercy,"—the battle of Worcester. But the varied embodiments of these, and of Mrs. Betty Arable ("the great fortune"), of Ephraim the Quaker, and the rest, are not all. The figures are set in their fitting environment; they ride their own horses, hallo to their own dogs, and eat and drink in their own dark-panelled rooms that look out on the pleached alleys of their ancient gardens. They live and move in their own passed-away atmosphere of association; and a faithful effort has moreover been

THE BALLAD OF BEAU BROCADE

AND OTHER POEMS

by Austin Dobson

Illustrated by

Hugh Thomson

with kindest regards
Hugh Thomson

PEN-SKETCHES ON THE HALF-TITLE OF "THE BALLAD OF
BEAU BROCADE."

made to realise each separate scene with strict relation to its text.

All of the "Coverley" series came out in the *English Illustrated.* So also did the designs for the next book, the *Coaching Days and Coaching Ways* of Mr. Outram Tristram, 1888. Here Mr. Thomson had a topographical collaborator, Mr. Herbert Railton, who did the major part of the very effective drawings in this kind. But Mr. Thomson's contributions may fairly be said to have exhausted the "romance" of the road. Inns and inn-yards, hosts and ostlers and chambermaids, stage-coachmen, toll-keepers, mail-coaches struggling in snow-drifts, mail-coaches held up by highwaymen, overturns, elopements, cast shoes, snapped poles, lost linch-pins, —all the episodes and moving accidents of bygone travel on the high road have abundant illustration, till the pages seem almost to reek of the stableyard, or ring with the horn.[1] And here it may be noted, as a peculiarity of Mr. Thomson's conscientious horse-drawing, that he depicts, not the ideal, but the actual animal. His steeds are not "faultless monsters" like the Dauphin's palfrey in *Henry the*

[1] Sometimes a literary or historical picture creeps into the text. Such are "Swift and Bolingbroke at Bucklebury" (p. 30); "Charles II. recognised by the Ostler" (p. 144), and "Barry Lyndon cracks a Bottle" (p. 116). *Barry Lyndon* with its picaresque note and Irish background, would seem an excellent contribution to the "Cranford" series. Why does not Mr. Thomson try his hand at it? He has illustrated *Esmond,* and the *Great Hoggarty Diamond.*

Fifth. They are "all sorts and conditions" of horses; and—if truth required it—would disclose as many sand-cracks as Rocinante, or as many equine defects (from wind-gall to the botts) as those imputed to that unhappy "Blackberry" sold by the Vicar of Wakefield at Welbridge Fair to Mr. Ephraim Jenkinson.

The *Vicar of Wakefield*—as it happens—was Mr. Thomson's next enterprise; and it is, in many respects, a most memorable one. It came out in December, 1890, having occupied him for nearly two years. He took exceptional pains to study and realise the several types for himself, and to ensure correctness of costume. From the first introductory procession of the Primrose family at the head of chapter i. to the awkward merriment of the two Miss Flamboroughs at the close, there is scarcely a page which has not some stroke of quiet fun, some graceful attitude, or some ingenious contrivance in composition. Considering that from Wenham's edition of 1780, nearly every illustrator of repute had tried his hand at Goldsmith's masterpiece in fiction,—that he had been attempted without humour by Stothard, without lightness by Mulready,[1]— that he had been made comic by Cruikshank, and vulgarised by Rowlandson,—it was certainly to Mr. Thomson's credit that he had approached his task

[1] Mulready's illustrations of 1843 are here referred to, not his pictures.

To
Austin Dobson
from Hugh Thomson
Decr 1899

Poet, Dramatist & Artist

PEN-SKETCH (TRIPLET) ON A FLY-LEAF OF "PEG WOFFINGTON."

with so much refinement, reverence and originality. If the book has a blemish, it is to be mentioned only because the artist, by his later practice, seems to have recognised it himself. For the purposes of process reproduction, the drawings were somewhat loaded and overworked.

This was not chargeable against the next volumes to be chronicled. Mrs. Gaskell's *Cranford*, 1891, and Miss Mitford's *Our Village*, 1893, are still regarded by many as the artist's happiest efforts. I say "still," because Mr. Thomson is only now in what Victor Hugo called the youth of old age (as opposed to the old age of youth); and it would be premature to assume that a talent so alert to multiply and diversify its efforts, had already attained the summit of its achievement. But in these two books he had certain unquestionable advantages. One obviously would be, that his audience were not already preoccupied by former illustrations; and he was consequently free to invent his own personages and follow his own fertile fancy, without recalling to that implacable and Gorgonising organ, the "Public Eye," any earlier pictorial conceptions. Another thing in his favour was, that in either case, the very definite, and not very complex types surrendered themselves readily to artistic embodiment. "It almost illustrated itself,"—he told an interviewer concerning *Cranford*; "the characters were so exquisitely and distinctly realised." Every one has known some like them; and the delightful Knutsford ladies (for "Cranford" was "Knutsford"), the "Boz"-loving Captain Brown and Mr. Holbrook, Peter and his father, and even Martha the maid, with their *mise en scène* of card-tables and crackle-china, and pattens and reticules, are part of the memories of our childhood. The same may be said of *Our Village,* except that the breath of Nature blows more freely through it than through the quiet Cheshire market-town; and there is a larger preponderance of those "charming glimpses of rural life" of which Lady Ritchie speaks admiringly in her sympathetic preface. And with regard to the "bits of scenery"—as Mr. Thomson himself calls them—it may be noted that one of the Manchester papers, speaking of *Cranford,* praised the artist's intimate knowledge of the locality, —a locality he had never seen. Most of his backgrounds were from sketches made on Wimbledon Common, near which—until he moved for a space to the ancient Cinque Port of Seaford in Sussex—he lived for the first years of his London life.

In strict order of time, Mr. Thomson's next important effort should have preceded the books of Miss Mitford and Mrs. Gaskell. The novels of Jane Austen—to which we now come—if not the artist's high-water mark, are certainly remarkable as a *tour de force*. To contrive some forty page

EVELINA AND THE BRANGHTONS.

(From Miss Burney's *Evelina*.)

illustrations for each of Miss Austen's admirable, but —from an illustrator's standpoint—not very palpitating productions,—with a scene usually confined to the dining-room or parlour,—with next to no animals, and with rare opportunities for landscape accessory,— was an "adventure"—in Cervantic phrase—which might well have given pause to a designer of less fertility and resource. But besides the figures there was the furniture; and acute admirers have pointed out that a nice discretion is exhibited in graduating the appointments of Longbourn and Netherfield Park,—of Rosings and Hunsford. But what is perhaps more worthy of remark is the artist's persistent attempt to give individuality, as well as grace, to his *dramatis personæ*. The unspeakable Mr. Collins, Mr. Bennet, the horsy Mr. John Thorpe, Mrs. Jennings and Mrs. Norris, the Eltons—are all carefully discriminated. Nothing can well be better than Mr. Woodhouse, with his "almost immaterial legs" drawn securely out of the range of a too-fierce fire, chatting placidly to Miss Bates upon the merits of water-gruel; nothing more in keeping than the Right Honourable Lady Catherine de Bourgh, "in the very torrent, tempest, and whirlwind" of her indignation, superciliously pausing to patronise the capabilities of the Longbourn reception rooms. Not less happy is the dumbfounded astonishment of Mrs. Bennet at her toilet, when she hears—to her stupefaction—that her daughter Elizabeth is to be mistress of Pemberley and ten thousand a year. This last is a head-piece; and it may be observed, as an additional difficulty in this group of novels, that, owing to the circumstances of publication, only in one of the books, *Pride and Prejudice*, was Mr. Thomson free to decorate the chapters with those ingenious *entêtes* and *culs-de-lampe* of which he so eminently possesses the secret.[1]

By this time his reputation had long been firmly established. To the Jane Austen volumes succeeded other numbers of the so-called "Cranford" series, to which, in 1894, Mr. Thomson had already added, under the title of *Coridon's Song and other Verses*, a fresh ingathering of old-time minstrelsy from the pages of the *English Illustrated*. Many of the drawings for these, though of necessity reduced for publication in book form, are in his most delightful and winning manner,—notably perhaps (if one must choose!) the martial ballad of that "Captain of Militia, Sir Dilberry Diddle," who

> —dreamt, Fame reports, that he cut all the throats
> Of the French as they landed in flat-bottomed boats

—or rather were going to land any time during the

---

[1] That eloquence of subsidiary detail, which has had so many exponents in English art from Hogarth onwards, is one of Mr. Thomson's most striking characteristics. The reader will find it exemplified in the beautiful book-plate at page 111, which, by the courtesy of its owner, Mr. Ernest Brown, I am permitted to reproduce.

LADY CASTLEWOOD AND HER SON.

(From Thackeray's *Esmond*.)

Seven Years' War. Excellent, too, are John Gay's ambling *Journey to Exeter*, the *Angler's Song* from Walton (which gives its name to the collection), and Fielding's rollicking "A-hunting we will go." Other "Cranford" books, which now followed, were James Lane Allen's *Kentucky Cardinal*, 1901; Fanny Burney's *Evelina*, 1903; Thackeray's *Esmond*, 1905; and two of George Eliot's novels—*Scenes of Clerical Life*, 1906, and *Silas Marner*, 1907. In 1899 Mr. Thomson had also undertaken another book for George Allen, an edition of Reade's *Peg Woffington*, —a task in which he took the keenest delight, particularly in the burlesque character of Triplet. These were all in the old pen-work; but some of the designs for *Silas Marner* were lightly and taste-fully coloured. This was a plan the author had adopted, with good effect, not only in a special edition of *Cranford* (1898), but for some of his original drawings which came into the market after exhibition. Nothing can be more seductive than a Hugh Thomson pen-sketch, when delicately tinted in sky-blue, *rose-Du Barry*, and apple-green (the *vert-pomme* dear—as Gautier says—to the soft moderns)—a treatment which lends them a subdued but indefinable distinction, as of old china with a pedigree, and fully justifies the amiable enthusiasm of the phrase-maker who described their inventor as the "Charles Lamb of illustration."

From the above enumeration certain omissions have of necessity been made. Besides the books mentioned, Mr. Thomson has contrived to prepare for newspapers and magazines many closely-studied sketches of contemporary manners. Some of the best of his work in this way is to be found in the late Mrs. E. T. Cook's *Highways and Byways of London Life,* 1902. For the *Highways and Byways* series, he has also illustrated, wholly or in part, volumes on Ireland, North Wales, Devon, Cornwall and Yorkshire. The last volume, Kent, 1907, is entirely decorated by himself. In this instance, his drawings throughout are in pencil, and he is his own topographer. It is a remarkable departure, both in manner and theme, though Mr. Thomson's liking for landscape has always been pronounced. "I would desire above all things," he told an interviewer, "to pass my time in painting landscape. Landscape pictures always attract me, and the grand examples, Gainsboroughs, Claudes, Cromes, and Turners, to be seen any day in our National Gallery, are a source of never-failing yearning and delight." The original drawings for the Kent book are of great beauty; and singularly dexterous in the varied methods by which the effect is produced. The artist is now at work on the county of Surrey. It is earnest of his versatility that, in 1904, he illustrated for Messrs. Wells, Darton and Co., with conspicuous

Mercery Lane

MERCERY LANE, CANTERBURY.

(From a pencil-drawing for *Highways and Byways in Kent*.)

success, a modernised prose version of certain of Chaucer's *Canterbury Tales,* as well as *Tales from Maria Edgeworth,* 1903; and he also executed, in 1892 and 1895,[1] some charming designs to selections from the verses of the present writer, who has long enjoyed the privilege of his friendship.

Personal traits do not come within the province of this paper, or it would be pleasant to dwell upon Mr. Thomson's modesty, his untiring industry, and his devotion to his art. But in regard to that art, it may be observed that to characterise it solely as "packing the memory with pleasant fancies" may suffice for an exordium, but is inadequate as a final appreciation. Let me therefore note down, as they occur to me, some of his more prominent pictorial characteristics. With three of the artists mentioned in this and the preceding paper, he has obvious affinities, while, in a sense, he includes them all. If he does not excel Stothard in the gift of grace, he does in range and variety; and he more than rivals him in composition. He has not, like Miss Greenaway, endowed the art-world with a special type of childhood; but his children are always life-like and engaging. (Compare, at a venture, the boy soldiers whom Frank Castlewood is drilling in chapter xi. of *Esmond,* or the delightful little fellow who is throwing up his arms in chapter ix. of

[1] *The Ballad of Beau Brocade,* and *The Story of Rosina.*

Emma). As regards dogs and horses and the rest, his colleague, Mr. Joseph Pennell, an expert critic, and a most accomplished artist, holds that he has "long since surpassed" Randolph Caldecott.[1] I doubt whether Mr. Thomson himself would concur with his eulogist in this. But he has assuredly followed Caldecott close; and in opulence of production which—as Macaulay insisted—should always count, has naturally exceeded that gifted, but short-lived, designer. If, pursuing an ancient practice, one were to attempt to label Mr. Thomson with a special distinction apart from, and in addition to, his other merits, I should be inclined to designate him the "Master of the Vignette,"—taking that word in its primary sense as including head-pieces, tail-pieces and initial letters. In this department, no draughts-man I can call to mind has ever shown greater fertility of invention, so much playful fancy, so much grace, so much kindly humour, and such a sane and wholesome spirit of fun.

[1] *Pen-Drawing and Pen-Draughtsmen*, 2nd ed. 1894, p. 358.

HORATIAN ODE
ON THE TERCENTENARY OF
"DON QUIXOTE"

HORATIAN ODE
ON THE TERCENTENARY OF "DON QUIXOTE"

(*Published at Madrid, by Francisco de Robles, January 1605*)

"Para mí sola nació don Quixote, y yo para él."—CERVANTES

ADVENTS we greet of great and small;
    Much we extol that may not live;
    Yet to the new-born Type we give
        No care at all!

This year,[1]—three centuries past,—by age
    More maimed than by LEPANTO's fight,—
    This year CERVANTES gave to light
        His matchless page,

Whence first outrode th' immortal Pair,—
    The half-crazed Hero and his hind,—
    To make sad laughter for mankind;
        And whence they fare

[1] *I.e.* January 1905.

Throughout all Fiction still, where chance
    Allies Life's dulness with its dreams—
    Allies what is, with what but seems,—
        Fact and Romance:—

O Knight of fire and Squire of earth!—
    O changing give-and-take between
    The aim too high, the aim too mean,
        I hail your birth,—

Three centuries past,—in sunburned SPAIN,
    And hang, on Time's PANTHEON wall,
    My votive tablet to recall
        That lasting gain!

THE BOOKS OF SAMUEL ROGERS

THE BOOKS OF SAMUEL ROGERS

ONE common grave, according to Garrick, covers the actor and his art. The same may be said of the raconteur. Oral tradition, or even his own writings, may preserve his precise words; but his peculiarities of voice or action, his tricks of utterance and intonation,—all the collateral details which serve to lend distinction or piquancy to the performance—perish irrevocably. The glorified gramophone of the future may perhaps rectify this for a new generation; and give us, without mechanical drawback, the authentic accents of speakers dead and gone; but it can never perpetuate the dramatic accompaniment of gesture and expression. If, as always, there are exceptions to this rule, they are necessarily evanescent. Now and then, it may be, some clever mimic will recall the manner of a passed-away predecessor; and he may even contrive to hand it on, more or less effectually, to a disciple. But the reproduction is of brief duration; and it is speedily effaced or transformed.

In this way it is, however, that we get our
most satisfactory idea of the once famous table-
talker, Samuel Rogers.   Charles Dickens, who sent
Rogers several of his books; who dedicated *Master
Humphrey's Clock* to him; and who frequently assisted
at the famous breakfasts in St. James's Place, was
accustomed—rather cruelly, it may be thought—to
take off his host's very characteristic way of telling a
story; and it is, moreover, affirmed by Mr. Percy
Fitzgerald[1] that, in the famous Readings, "the
strangely obtuse and owl-like expression, and the
slow, husky croak" of Mr. Justice Stareleigh in the
"Trial from *Pickwick*," were carefully copied from
the author of the *Pleasures of Memory*.   That
Dickens used thus to amuse his friends is confirmed
by the autobiography of the late Frederick Locker,[2]
who perfectly remembered the old man, to see whom
he had been carried, as a boy, by his father.   He had
also heard Dickens repeat one of Rogers's stock
anecdotes (it was that of the duel in a dark room,
where the more considerate combatant, firing up
the chimney, brings down his adversary) ;[3]—and he
speaks of Dickens as mimicking Rogers's "calm, low-
pitched, drawling voice and dry biting manner very

---

[1] *Recreations of a Literary Man,* 1882, p. 137.

[2] *My Confidences,* by Frederick Locker-Lampson, 1896, pp. 98 and 325.

[3] The duellists were an Englishman and a Frenchman; and Rogers was
in the habit of adding as a postscript: "When I tell that in Paris, I always
put the Englishman up the chimney!"

comically."[1] At the same time, it must be remembered
that these reminiscences relate to Rogers in his old
age. He was over seventy when Dickens published
his first book, *Sketches by Boz*; and, though it is
possible that Rogers's voice was always rather
sepulchral, and his enunciation unusually deliberate
and monotonous, he had nevertheless, as Locker says,
"made story-telling a fine art." Continued practice
had given him the utmost economy of words; and
as far as brevity and point are concerned, his method
left nothing to be desired. Many of his best efforts
are still to be found in the volume of *Table-Talk*
edited for Moxon in 1856 by the Rev. Alexander
Dyce; or preferably, as actually written down by
Rogers himself in the delightful *Recollections* issued
three years later by his nephew and executor, William
Sharpe.

But although the two things are often intimately
connected, the "books," and not the "stories" of
Rogers, are the subject of the present paper. After
this, it sounds paradoxical to have to admit that his
reputation as a connoisseur far overshadowed his reputation as a bilbliophile. When, in December 1855,
he died, his pictures and curios,—his "articles of virtue and bigotry" as a modern Malaprop would have
styled them,—attracted far more attention than the not

---

[1] It may be added that Mr. Percy Fitzgerald, himself no mean mime,
may be sometimes persuaded to imitate Dickens imitating Rogers.

very numerous volumes forming his library.[1] What
people flocked to see at the tiny treasure-house over-
looking the Green Park,[2] which its nonegenarian
owner had occupied for more than fifty years, were
the "Puck" and "Strawberry Girl" of Sir Joshua,
the Titians, Giorgiones, and Guidos,[3] the Poussins
and Claudes, the drawings of Raphael and Dürer and
Lucas van Leyden, the cabinet decorated by Stothard,
the chimney-piece carved by Flaxman; the miniatures
and bronzes and Etruscan vases,—all the "infinite
riches in a little room," which crowded No. 22 from
garret to basement. These were the rarities that
filled the columns of the papers and the voices of the
quidnuncs when in 1856 they came to the hammer.
But although the Press of that day takes careful
count of these things, it makes little reference to the
sale of the "books" of the banker-bard who spent
some £15,000 on the embellishments of his *Italy*
and his *Poems*; and although Dr. Burney says that
Rogers's library included "the best editions of the
best authors in most languages," he had clearly no
widespread reputation as a book-collector pure and
simple. Nevertheless he loved his books,—that is,

---

[1] The prices obtained confirm this. The total sum realised was
£45,188:14:3. Of this the books represented no more than £1415:5.

[2] This—with its triple range of bow-windows, from one of which Rogers
used to watch his favourite sunsets—is now the residence of Lord
Northcliffe.

[3] Three of these—the *"Noli me tangere"* of Titian, Giorgione's "Knight
in Armour," and Guido's *"Ecce Homo"*—are now in the National Gallery,
to which they were bequeathed by Rogers.

he loved the books he read. And, as far as can be ascertained, he anticipated the late Master of Balliol, since he read only the books he liked. Nor was he ever diverted from his predilections by mere fashion or novelty. "He followed Bacon's maxim"—says one who knew him—"to read much, not many things: *multum legere, non multa.* He used to say, 'When a new book comes out, I read an old one.' "[1]

The general Rogers-sale at Christie's took place in the spring of 1856, and twelve days had been absorbed before the books were reached. Their sale took six days more—*i.e.* from May 12 to May 19. As might be expected from Rogers's traditional position in the literary world, the catalogue contains many presentation copies. What, at first sight, would seem the earliest, is the *Works* of Edward Moore, 1796, 2 vols. But if this be the fabulist and editor of the *World,* it can scarcely have been received from the writer, since, in 1796, Moore had been dead for nearly forty years. With Bloomfield's poems of 1802, l. p., we are on surer ground, for Rogers, like Capel Lofft, had been kind to the author of *The Farmer's Boy,* and had done his best to obtain him a pension. Another early tribute, subsequently followed by the *Tales of the Hall,* was Crabbe's *Borough,* which he sent to Rogers in 1810, in response to polite overtures

---

[1] *Edinburgh Review,* vol. civ. p. 105, by Abraham Hayward.

made to him by the poet. This was the beginning of a lasting friendship, of no small import to Crabbe, as it at once admitted him to Rogers's circle, an advantage of which there are many traces in Crabbe's journal. Next comes Madame de Staël's much proscribed *De l'Allemagne* (the Paris edition); and from its date, 1813, it must have been presented to Rogers when its irrepressible author was in England. She often dined or breakfasted at St. James's Place, where (according to Byron), she outtalked Whitbread, confounded Sir Humphry Davy, and was herself well "*ironed*"[1] by Sheridan. Rogers considered *Corinne* to be her best novel, and *Delphine* a terrible falling-off. The Germany he found "very fatiguing." "She writes her works four or five times over, correcting them only in that way"—he says. "The end of a chapter [is] always the most obscure, as she ends with an epigram."[2] Another early presentation copy is the second edition of Bowles's *Missionary*, 1815. According to Rogers, who claims to have suggested the poem, it was to have been inscribed to him. But somehow or other, the book got dedicated to

---

[1] Perhaps a remembrance of Mrs. Slipslop's "*ironing.*"

[2] Clayden's *Rogers and his Contemporaries*, 1889, i. 225. As an epigrammatist himself, Rogers might have been more indulgent to a *consœur.* Here is one of Madame de Staël's "ends of chapters":—*La monotonie, dans la retraite, tranquillise l'âme; la monotonie, dans le grand monde, fatigue l'esprit*" (ch. viii.). But he evidently found her rather overpowering.

a noble lord who—Rogers adds drily—never, either by word or letter, made any acknowledgment of the homage.[1] It is not impossible that there is some confusion of recollection here, or Rogers is misreported by Dyce. The first anonymous edition of the *Missionary,* 1813, had *no* dedication; and the second was inscribed to the Marquess of Lansdowne because he had been prominent among those who recognised the merit of its predecessor.

Several of Scott's poems, with Rogers's autograph, and Scott's card, appear in the catalogue; and, in 1812, Byron, who a year after inscribed the *Giaour* to Rogers, sent him the first two cantos of *Childe Harold.* In 1838, Moore presents *Lalla Rookh,* with Heath's plates, a work which, upon its first appearance, twenty years earlier, had been dedicated to Rogers. In 1839 Charles Dickens followed with *Nicholas Nickleby,* succeeded a year later by *Master Humphrey's Clock* (1840-1), also dedicated to Rogers in recognition, not only of his poetical merit, but of his "active sympathy with the poorest and humblest of his kind." Rogers was fond of "Little Nell"; and in the Preface to *Barnaby Rudge,* Dickens gracefully acknowledged that "for a beautiful thought" in the seventy-second chapter of the *Old Curiosity Shop,* he was indebted to Rogers's Ginevra in the *Italy* :—

[1] *Table-Talk*, 1856, p. 258.

And long might'st thou have seen
An old man wandering *as in quest of something,*
Something he could not find—he knew not what.

The *American Notes,* 1842, was a further offering
from Dickens. Among other gifts may be noted
Wordsworth's *Poems,* 1827-35; Campbell's *Pilgrim
of Glencoe,* 1842; Longfellow's *Ballads* and *Voices
of the Night,* 1840-2; Macaulay's *Lays* and
Tennyson's *Poems,* 1842; and lastly, Hazlitt's
Criticisms on Art, 1844, and Carlyle's *Letters and
Speeches of Cromwell,* 1846. Brougham's philosophical novel of *Albert Lunel; or, the Château of
Languedoc,* 3 vols. 1844, figures in the catalogue
as "withdrawn." It had been suppressed "for
private reasons" upon the eve of publication; and
this particular copy being annotated by Rogers (to
whom it was inscribed) those concerned were no
doubt all the more anxious that it should not get
abroad. Inspection of the reprint of 1872 shows,
however, that want of interest was its chief error.
A reviewer of 1858 roundly calls it "feeble" and
"commonplace"; and it could hardly have increased
its writer's reputation. Indeed, by some, it was not
supposed to be from his Lordship's pen at all.
Rogers, it may be added, frequently annotated his
books. His copies of Pope, Gray and Scott had many
marginalia. Clarke's and Fox's histories of James II.
were also works which he decorated in this way.

As already hinted, not very many bibliographical curiosities are included in the St. James's
Place collection; and to look for Shakespeare
quartos or folios, for example, would be idle.
Ordinary editions of Shakespeare, such as Johnson's
and Theobald's; Shakespeariana, such as Mrs.
Montagu's *Essay* and Ayscough's *Index,*—these are
there of course. If the list also takes in Thomas
Caldecott's *Hamlet,* and *As you like it* (1832), that
is, first, because the volume is a presentation copy;
and secondly, because Caldecott's colleague in his
frustrate enterprise was Crowe, Rogers's Miltonic
friend, hereafter mentioned. Rogers's own feeling
for Shakespeare was cold and hypercritical; and
he was in the habit of endorsing with emphasis
Ben Jonson's aspiration that the master had blotted
a good many of his too-facile lines. Nevertheless,
it is possible to pick out a few exceptional volumes
from Mr. Christie's record. Among the earliest
comes a copy of Garth's *Dispensary,* 1703, which
certainly boasts an illustrious pedigree. Pope, who
received it from the author, had carefully corrected
it in several places; and in 1744 bequeathed it to
Warburton. Warburton, in his turn, handed it on
to Mason, from whom it descended to Lord St.
Helens, by whom, again, shortly before his death
(1815), it was presented to Rogers. To Pope's
corrections, which Garth adopted, Mason had added

a comment. What made the volume of further
interest was, that it contained Lord Dorchester's
receipt for his subscription to Pope's *Homer*; and,
inserted at the end, a full-length portrait of Pope;
viz., that engraved in Warton's edition of 1797, as
sketched in pen-and-ink by William Hoare of Bath.
Another interesting item is the quarto first edition
(the first three books) of Spenser's *Faerie Queene,*
Ponsonbie, 1590: and a third, the *Paradise Lost*
of Milton in ten books, the original text of 1667
(with the 1669 title-page and the Argument and
Address to the Reader)—both bequeathed to Rogers
by W. Jackson of Edinburgh. (One of the stock
exhibits at "Memory Hall"—as 22 St. James's
Place was playfully called by some of the owner's
friends—was Milton's receipt to Symmons the
printer for the five pounds he received for his
epic. This, framed and glazed, hung, according to
Lady Eastlake, on one of the doors).[1] A fourth
rare book was William Bonham's black-letter Chaucer,
a folio which had been copiously annotated in MS.
by Horne Tooke, who gave it to Rogers. It moreover contained, at folio 221, the record of Tooke's

[1] It was, no doubt, identical with the "Original Articles of Agreement"
(Add. MSS. 18,861) between Milton and Samuel Symmons, printer,
dated 27th April, 1667, presented by Rogers in 1852 to the British Museum.
Besides the above-mentioned £5 down, there were to be three further
payments of £5 each on the sale of three editions, each of 1300 copies.
The second edition appeared in 1674, the year of the author's death.

arrest at Wimbledon on 16th May, 1794, and subsequent committal on the 19th to the Tower, for alleged high treason.[1] Further *notabilia* in this category were the Duke of Marlborough's *Hypnero-tomachie* of Poliphilus, Paris, 1554, and also the Aldine edition of 1499; the very rare 1572 issue of Camoens's *Lusiads*; Holbein's *Dance of Death*, the Lyons issues of 1538 and 1547; first editions of Bewick's *Birds* and *Quadrupeds*; Le Sueur's *Life of St. Bruno*, with the autograph of Sir Joshua Reynolds, and a rare quarto (1516) of Boccaccio's *Decameron*.

But the mere recapitulation of titles readily grows tedious, even to the elect; and I turn to some of the volumes with which, from references in the *Table-Talk* and *Recollections*, their owner might seem to be more intimately connected. Foremost among these—one would think—should come his own productions. Most of these, no doubt, are included under the auctioneers' heading of "Works and Illus-trations." In the "Library" proper, however, there

---

[1] He was acquitted. His notes, in pencil, and relating chiefly to his *Diversions of Purley,* were actually written in the Tower. Rogers, who was present at the trial in November, mentioned, according to Dyce, a curious incident bearing upon a now obsolete custom referred to by Goldsmith and others. As usual, the prisoner's dock, in view of possible jail-fever, was strewn with sweet-smelling herbs—fennel, rosemary and the like. Tooke indignantly swept them away. Another of several char-acteristic anecdotes told by Rogers of Tooke is as follows:—Being asked once at college what his father was, he replied, "A Turkey Merchant." Tooke *père* was a poulterer in Clare Market.

are few traces of them. There is a quarto copy of
the unfortunate *Columbus,* with Stothard's sketches;
and there is the choice little *Pleasures of Memory*
of 1810, with Luke Clennell's admirable cuts in
facsimile from the same artist's pen-and-ink,—a
volume which, come what may, will always hold its
own in the annals of book-illustration. That there
were more than one of these latter may be an
accident. Rogers, nevertheless, like many book-
lovers, must have indulged in duplicates. According
to Hayward, once at breakfast, when some one quoted
Gray's irresponsible outburst concerning the novels
of Marivaux and Crébillon *le fils,* Rogers asked his
guests, three in number, whether they were familiar
with Marivaux's *Vie de Marianne,* a book which he
himself confesses to have read through six times,
and which French critics still hold, on inconclusive
evidence, to have been the "only begetter" of
Richardson's *Pamela* and the sentimental novel.
None of the trio knew anything about it. "Then
I will lend you each a copy," rejoined Rogers; and
the volumes were immediately produced, doubtless
by that faithful and indefatigable factotum, Edmund
Paine, of whom his master was wont to affirm that
he would not only find any book *in* the house,
but *out* of it as well. What is more (unless it be
assumed that the poet's stock was larger still), one,
at least, of the three copies must have been returned,

since there is a copy in the catalogue. As might
be expected in the admirer of Marivaux's heroine,
the list is also rich in Jean-Jacques, whose "*goût vif
pour les déjeuners,*" this Amphitryon often extolled,
quoting with approval Rousseau's opinion that "*C'est
le temps de la journée où nous sommes le plus tran-
quilles, où nous causons le plus à notre aise.*" Another
of his favourite authors was Manzoni, whose *Promessi
Sposi* he was inclined to think he would rather have
written than all Scott's novels; and he never tired
of reading Louis Racine's *Mémoires* of his father,
1747,—that "*filon de l'or pur du dix-septième siècle*"
—as Villemain calls it—"*qui se prolonge dans l'âge
suivant.*" Some of Rogers's likings sound strange
enough nowadays. With Campbell, he delighted
in Cowper's *Homer,* which he assiduously studied,
and infinitely preferred to that of Pope. Into
Chapman's it must be assumed that he had not
looked—certainly he has left no sonnet on the
subject. Milton was perhaps his best-loved bard.
"When I was travelling in Italy (he says), I made
two authors my constant study for versification,—
Milton *and Crowe.*" (The italics are ours.) It is
an odd collocation; but not unintelligible. William
Crowe, the now forgotten Public Orator of Oxford,
and author of *Lewesdon Hill,* was an intimate friend;
a writer on versification; and, last but not least,
a very respectable echo of the Miltonic note, as

the following, from a passage dealing with the loss
in 1786 of the *Halsewell* East Indiaman off the
coast of Dorset, sufficiently testifies:—

> The richliest-laden ship
> Of spicy Ternate, or that annual sent
> To the Philippines o'er the southern main
> From Acapulco, carrying massy gold,
> Were poor to this;—freighted with hopeful Youth
> And Beauty, and high Courage undismay'd
> By mortal terrors, and paternal Love, etc., etc.

It is not improbable that Rogers caught the mould
of his blank verse from the copy rather than from
the model. In the matter of style—as Flaubert has
said—the second-bests are often the better teachers.
More is to be learned from La Fontaine and Gautier
than from Molière and Victor Hugo.

Many art-books, many books addressed specially
to the connoisseur, as well as most of those invalu-
able volumes no gentleman's library should be without, found their places on Rogers's hospitable shelves.
Of such, it is needless to speak; nor, in this place,
is it necessary to deal with his finished and amiable,
but not very vigorous or vital poetry. A parting
word may, however, be devoted to the poet himself.
Although, during his lifetime, and particularly
towards its close, his weak voice and singularly
blanched appearance exposed him perpetually to a
kind of brutal personality now happily tabooed,

it cannot be pretended that, either in age or youth, he was an attractive-looking man. In these cases, as in that of Goldsmith, a measure of burlesque sometimes provides a surer criterion than academic portraiture. The bust of the sculptor-caricaturist, Danton, is of course what even Hogarth would have classed as *outré* [1]; but there is reason for believing that Maclise's sketch in *Fraser* of the obtrusively bald, cadaverous and wizened figure in its arm-chair, which gave such a shudder of premonition to Goethe, and which Maginn, reflecting the popular voice, declared to be a mortal likeness—"painted to the very death"—was more like the original than his pictures by Lawrence and Hoppner. One can comprehend, too, that the person whom nature had so ungenerously endowed, might be perfectly capable of retorting to rudeness, or the still-smarting recollection of rudeness, with those weapons of mordant wit and acrid epigram which are not unfrequently the protective compensation of physical shortcomings. But this conceded, there are numberless anecdotes which testify to Rogers's cultivated taste and real good breeding, to his genuine benevolence, to his almost sentimental craving for appreciation and affection. In a paper on his books, it is permissible to end with

[1] Rogers's own copy of this, which (it may be added), he held in horror, now belongs to Mr. Edmund Gosse. Lord Londonderry has a number of Danton's busts.

K

a bookish anecdote. One of his favourite memories, much repeated in his latter days, was that of Cowley's laconic Will,—"I give my body to the earth, and my soul to my Maker." Lady Eastlake shall tell the rest:—"This . . . . proved on one occasion too much for one of the party, and in an incautious moment a flippant young lady exclaimed, 'But, Mr. Rogers, what of Cowley's *property*?' An ominous silence ensued, broken only by a *sotto voce* from the late Mrs. Procter: 'Well, my dear, you have put your foot in it; no more invitations for you in a hurry.' But she did the kind old man, then above ninety, wrong. The culprit continued to receive the same invitations and the same welcome."[1]

[1] *Quarterly Review*, vol. 167, p. 512.

PEPYS' "DIARY"

PEPYS' "DIARY"

To One who asked why he wrote it

You ask me what was his intent?
    In truth, I'm not a German;
'Tis plain though that he neither meant
    A Lecture nor a Sermon.

But there it is,—the thing's a Fact.
    I find no other reason
But that some scribbling itch attacked
    Him in and out of season,

To write what no one else should read,
    With this for second meaning,
To "cleanse his bosom" (and indeed
    It sometimes wanted cleaning);

To speak, as 'twere, his private mind,
    Unhindered by repression,
To make his motley life a kind
    Of Midas' ears confession;

And thus outgrew this work *per se,*—
    This queer, kaleidoscopic,
Delightful, blabbing, vivid, free
    Hotch-pot of daily topic,

So artless in its vanity,
    So fleeting, so eternal,
So packed with "poor Humanity"—
    We know as Pepys' his journal.[1]

[1] Written for the Pepys' Dinner at Magdalene College, Cambridge, February 23rd, 1905.

A FRENCH CRITIC ON BATH

A FRENCH CRITIC ON BATH

AMONG other pleasant premonitions of the present *entente cordiale* between France and England is the increased attention which, for some time past, our friends of Outre Manche have been devoting to our literature. That this is wholly of recent growth, is not, of course, to be inferred. It must be nearly five-and-forty years since M. Hippolyte Taine issued his logical and orderly *Histoire de la Littérature Anglaise*; while other isolated efforts of insight and importance—such as the *Laurence Sterne* of M. Paul Stapfer, and the excellent *Le Public et les Hommes de Lettres en Angleterre au XVIIIe Siècle* of the late M. Alexandre Beljame of the Sorbonne—are already of distant date. But during the last two decades the appearance of similar productions has been more recurrent and more marked. From one eminent writer alone—M. J.-J. Jusserand—we have received an entire series of studies of exceptional charm, variety, and accomplishment. M. Felix Rabbe has given us a sympathetic analysis of Shelley; M. Auguste Angellier,—himself a poet of individuality

and distinction,—what has been rightly described
as a "splendid work" on Burns;[1] while M. Émile
Legouis, in a minute examination of "The Prelude,"
has contrasted and compared the orthodox Wordsworth of maturity with the juvenile semi-atheist of
Coleridge. Travelling farther afield, M. W. Thomas
has devoted an exhaustive volume to Young of
the *Night Thoughts*; M. Léon Morel, another to
Thomson; and, incidentally, a flood of fresh light
has been thrown upon the birth and growth of
the English Novel by the admirable *Jean-Jacques
Rousseau et les Origines du Cosmopolitisme Littéraire*
of the late Joseph Texte—an investigation unquestionably of the ripest scholarship, and the most
extended research. And now once more there are
signs that French lucidity and French precision
are about to enter upon other conquests; and
we have M. Barbeau's study of a famous old
English watering-place[2]—appropriately dedicated,
as is another of the books already mentioned, to
M. Beljame.[3]

---

[1] A volume of *Pages Choisies de Auguste Angellier, Prose et Vers,*
with an Introduction by M. Legouis, has recently (1908) been issued by
the Clarendon Press. It contains lengthy extracts from M. Angellier's
study of Burns.

[2] *Une Ville d'Eaux Anglaise ou XVIIIᵉ Siècle. La Société Elégante
et Littéraire à Bath sous la Reine Anne et sous les Georges.* Par A.
Barbeau. Paris, Picard, 1904.

[3] The list grows apace. To the above, among others, must now be
added M. René Huchon's brilliant little essay on Mrs. Montagu, and his
elaborate study of Crabbe, to say nothing of M. Jules Derocquigny's
Lamb, M. Jules Douady's Hazlitt, and M. Joseph Aynard's Coleridge.

At first sight, topography, even when combined with social sketches, may seem less suited to a foreigner and an outsider than it would be to a resident and a native. In the attitude of the latter to the land in which he lives or has been born, there is always an inherent something of the soil for which even trained powers of comparison, and a special perceptive faculty, are but imperfect substitutes. On the other hand, the visitor from over-sea is, in many respects, better placed for observation than the inhabitant. He enjoys not a little—it has been often said—of the position of posterity. He takes in more at a glance; he leaves out less; he is disturbed by no apprehensions of explaining what is obvious, or discovering what is known. As a consequence, he sets down much which, from long familiarity, an indigenous critic would be disposed to discard, although it might not be, in itself, either uninteresting or superfluous. And if, instead of dealing with the present and actual, his concern is with history and the past, his external standpoint becomes a strength rather than a weakness. He can survey his subject with a detachment which is wholly favourable to his project; and he can give it, with less difficulty than another, the advantages of scientific treatment and an artistic setting. Finally, if his theme have definite limits—as for instance an appreciable beginning, middle, and end—he must be held to be exceptionally fortunate. And this, either from happy guessing, or sheer good luck, is M. Barbeau's case. All these conditions are present in the annals of the once popular pleasure-resort of which he has elected to tell the story. It arose gradually; it grew through a century of unexampled prosperity; it sank again to the level of a country-town. If it should ever arise again,—and it is by no means a *ville morte*,— it will be in an entirely different way. The particular Bath of the eighteenth century—the Bath of Queen Anne and the Georges, of Nash and Fielding and Sheridan, of Anstey and Mrs. Siddons, of Wesley and Lady Huntingdon, of Quin and Gainsborough and Lawrence and a hundred others—is no more. It is a case of *Fuit Ilium*. It has gone for ever; and can never be revived in the old circumstances. To borrow an apposite expression from M. Texte, it is an organism whose evolution has accomplished its course.

M. Barbeau's task, then, is very definitely mapped-out and circumscribed. But he is far too good a craftsman to do no more than give a mere panorama of that daily Bath programme which King Nash and his dynasty ordained and established. He goes back to the origins; to the legend of King Lear's leper-father; to the *Diary* of the too-much-neglected Celia Fiennes; to Pepys[1] and Grammont's

[1] Oddly enough—if M. Barbeau's index is to be trusted, and it is an

Memoirs; to the days when hapless Catherine of
Braganza, with the baleful *"belle* Stewart" in her
train, made fruitless pilgrimage to Bladud's spring as
a remedy against sterility. He sketches, with due
acknowledgments to Goldsmith's unique little book,
the biography of that archquack, *poseur,* and very
clever organiser, Mr. Richard Nash, the first real
Master of the Ceremonies; and he gives a full
account of his followers and successors. He also
minutely relates the story of Sheridan's marriage to
his beautiful "St. Cecilia," Elizabeth Ann Linley.
A separate and very interesting chapter is allotted to
Lady Huntingdon and the Methodists, not without
levies from the remarkable *Spiritual Quixote* of that
Rev. Richard Graves of Claverton, of whom an
excellent account was given not long since in Mr.
W. H. Hutton's suggestive *Burford Papers.* Other
chapters are occupied with Bath and its *belles lettres*;
with "Squire Allworthy" of Prior Park and his
literary guests, Pope, Warburton, Fielding and his
sister, etc.; with the historic Frascati vase of Lady
Miller at Batheaston, which stirred the ridicule of
Horace Walpole, and is still, it is said, to be seen in

unusually good one,—he makes no reference to Evelyn's visit to Bath.
But Evelyn went there in June, 1654, bathed in the Cross Bath, criticised
the *"facciata"* of the Abbey Church, complained of the "narrow, uneven
and unpleasant streets," and inter-visited with the company frequenting
the place for health. "Among the rest of the idle diversions of the town,"
he says, "one musician was famous for acting a changeling [idiot or
half-wit], which indeed he personated strangely." (*Diary,* Globe edn.,
1908, p. 174.)

a local park. The closing pages treat of Bath—musical, artistic, scientific—of its gradual transformation as a health resort—of its eventual and fore-doomed decline and fall as the one fashionable watering-place, supreme and single, for Great Britain and Ireland.

But it is needless to prolong analysis. One's only wonder—as usual after the event—is that what has been done so well had never been thought of before. For, while M. Barbeau is to be congratulated upon the happy task he has undertaken, we may also congratulate ourselves that he has performed it so effectively. His material is admirably arranged. He has supported it by copious notes; and he has backed it up by an impressive bibliography of authorities ancient and modern. This is something; but it is not all.[1] He has done much more than this. He has contrived that, in his picturesque and learned pages, the old "Queen of the West" shall live again, with its circling terraces, its grey stone houses and ill-paved streets, its crush of chairs and chariots, its throng of smirking, self-satisfied promenaders. One seems to see the clumsy stage-coaches depositing their touzled and tumbled inmates, in their rough rocklows and quaint travelling headgear, at the "Bear" or the "White Hart," after a jolting

[1] To the English version (Heinemann, 1904) an eighteenth-century map of Bath, and a number of interesting views and portraits have been added.

two or three days' journey from Oxford or London, not without the usual experiences, real and imaginary, of suspicious-looking horsemen at Hounslow, or masked "gentlemen of the pad" on Claverton Down. One hears the peal of five-and-twenty bells which greets the arrival of visitors of importance; and notes the obsequious and venal town-waits who follow them to their lodgings in Gay Street or Milsom Street or the Parades,—where they will, no doubt, be promptly attended by the Master of the Ceremonies, "as fine as fivepence," and a very pretty, sweet-smelling gentleman, to be sure, whether his name be Wade or Derrick. Next day will probably discover them in chip hats and flannel, duly equipped with wooden bowls and bouquets, at the King's Bath, where, through a steaming atmosphere, you may survey their artless manœuvres (as does Lydia Melford in *Humphry Clinker*) from the windows of the Pump Room, to which rallying-place they will presently repair to drink the waters, in a medley of notables and notorieties, members of Parliament, chaplains and led-captains, Noblemen with ribbons and stars, dove-coloured Quakers, Duchesses, quacks, fortune-hunters, lackeys, lank-haired Methodists, Bishops, and boarding-school misses. Ferdinand Count Fathom will be there, as well as my Lord Ogleby; Lady Bellaston (and Mr. Thomas Jones) ; Geoffry Wildgoose and Tugwell the

cobbler; Lismahago and Tabitha Bramble; the caustic
Mrs. Selwyn and the blushing Miss Anville. Be certain, too, that, sooner or later, you will encounter Mrs.
Candour and Lady Sneerwell, Sir Benjamin Backbite
and his uncle, Mr. Crabtree, for this is their main
haunt and region—in fact, they were born here.
You may follow this worshipful and piebald procession to the Public Breakfasts in the Spring Gardens, to
the Toy-shops behind the Church, to the Coffee-houses
in Westgate Street, to the Reading Rooms on the
Walks, where, in Mr. James Leake's parlour at the
back—if you are lucky—you may behold the celebrated Mr. Ralph Allen of Prior Park, talking either
to Mr. Henry Fielding or to Mr. Leake's brother-
in-law, Mr. Samuel Richardson, but never—if we are
correctly informed—to both of them together. Or
you may run against Mr. Christopher Anstey of the
over-praised *Guide*, walking arm-in-arm with another
Bathonian, Mr. Melmoth, whose version of Pliny
was once held to surpass its original. At the Abbey
—where there are daily morning services—you shall
listen to the silver periods of Bishop Hurd, whom
his admirers call fondly "the Beauty of Holiness";
at St. James's you can attend the full-blown lectures,
"more unctuous than ever he preached," of Bishop
Beilby Porteus; or you may succeed in procuring a
card for a select hearing, at Edgar Buildings, of Lady
Huntingdon's eloquent chaplain, Mr. Whitefield.

With the gathering shades of even, you may pass, if so minded, to Palmer's Theatre in Orchard Street, and follow Mrs. Siddons acting Belvidera in Otway's *Venice Preserv'd* to the Pierre of that forgotten Mr. Lee whom Fanny Burney put next to Garrick; or you may join the enraptured audience whom Mrs. Jordan is delighting with her favourite part of Priscilla Tomboy in *The Romp*. You may assist at the concerts of Signor Venanzio Rauzzini and Monsieur La Motte; you may take part in a long minuet or country dance at the Upper or Lower Assembly Rooms, which Bunbury will caricature; you may even lose a few pieces at the green tables; and, should you return home late enough, may watch a couple of stout chairmen at the door of the "Three Tuns" in Stall Street, hoisting that seasoned toper, Mr. James Quin, into a sedan after his evening's quantum of claret. What you do to-day, you will do to-morrow, if the bad air of the Pump Room has not given you a headache, or the waters a touch of vertigo; and you will continue to do it for a month or six weeks, when the lumbering vehicle with the leathern straps and crane-necked springs will carry you back again over the deplorable roads ("so *sidelum* and *jumblum*," one traveller calls them) to your town-house, or your country-box, or your city-shop or chambers, as the case may be. Here, in due course, you will begin

L

to meditate upon your next excursion to THE BATH, provided always that you have not dipped your estate at "E.O.", or been ruined by milliners' bills;—that your son has not gone northwards with a sham Scotch heiress, or your daughter been married at Charlcombe, by private license, to a pinchbeck Irish peer. For all these things—however painful the admission—were, according to the most credible chroniclers, the by-no-means infrequent accompaniment or sequel of an unguarded sojourn at the old jigging, card-playing, scandal-loving, pleasure-seeking city in the loop of "the soft-flowing Avon."

It is an inordinate paragraph, outraging all known rules of composition! But then—How seductive a subject is eighteenth-century Bath!—and how rich in memories is M. Barbeau's book!

A WELCOME FROM THE
"JOHNSON CLUB"

A WELCOME FROM THE "JOHNSON CLUB"

To William John Courthope, *March* 12, 1903

WHEN POPE came back from Trojan wars once more,
He found a Bard, to meet him on the shore,
And hail his advent with a strain as clear
As e'er was sung by BYRON or by FRERE.[1]

You, SIR, have travelled from no distant clime,
Yet would JOHN GAY could welcome you in rhyme;
And by some fable not too coldly penned,
Teach how with judgment one may praise a Friend.

There is no need that I should tell in words
Your prowess from *The Paradise of Birds*;[2]
No need to show how surely you have traced
The Life in Poetry, the Law in Taste;[3]

[1] *Alexander Pope: his Safe Return from Troy. A Congratulatory Poem on his Completing his Translation of Homer's Iliad.* (In *ottava rima.*) By Mr. Gay, 1720(?). Frere's burlesque, *Monks and Giants*—it will be remembered—set the tune to Byron's *Beppo.*
[2] *The Paradise of Birds*, 1870.
[3] *Life in Poetry, Law in Taste,* two series of Lectures delivered in Oxford, 1895-1900, 1901.

Or mark with what unwearied strength you wear
The weight that WARTON found too great to bear.[1]
There is no need for this or that.   My plan
Is less to laud the Matter than the Man.

This is my brief.   We recognise in you
The mind judicial, the untroubled view;
The critic who, without pedantic pose,
Takes his firm foothold on the thing he knows;
Who, free alike from passion or pretence,
Holds the good rule of calm and common sense;
And be the subject or perplexed or plain,—
Clear or confusing,—is throughout urbane,
Patient, persuasive, logical, precise,
And only hard to vanity and vice.

More I could add, but brevity is best;—
These are our claims to honour you as Guest.

[1] *A History of English Poetry,* 1895 (in progress).

THACKERAY'S "ESMOND"

THACKERAY'S "ESMOND"

AT this date, Thackeray's *Esmond* has passed from the domain of criticism into that securer region where the classics, if they do not actually "slumber out their immortality," are at least preserved from profane intrusion. This "noble story"[1]—as it was called by one of its earliest admirers—is no longer, in any sense, a book "under review." The painful student of the past may still, indeed, with tape and compass, question its details and proportions; or the quick-fingered professor of paradox, jauntily turning it upside-down, rejoice in the results of his perverse dexterity; but certain things are now established in regard to it, which cannot be gainsaid, even by those who assume the superfluous office of anatomising the accepted. In the first place, if *Esmond* be not the author's greatest work (and there are those who, like the late Anthony Trollope, would willingly give it that rank), it is unquestionably

[1] "Never could I have believed that Thackeray, great as his abilities are, could have written so noble a story as *Esmond*."—WALTER SAVAGE LANDOR, August 1856.

his greatest work in its particular kind, for its sequel, *The Virginians*, however admirable in detached passages, is desultory and invertebrate, while *Denis Duval*, of which the promise was great, remains unfinished. With *Vanity Fair*, the author's masterpiece in another manner, *Esmond* cannot properly be compared, because an imitation of the past can never compete in verisimilitude or on any satisfactory terms with a contemporary picture. Nevertheless, in its successful reproduction of the tone of a bygone epoch, lies *Esmond's* second and incontestable claim to length of days. Although fifty years and more have passed since it was published, it is still unrivalled as the typical example of that class of historical fiction, which, dealing indiscriminately with characters real and feigned, develops them both with equal familiarity, treating them each from within, and investing them impartially with a common atmosphere of illusion. No modern novel has done this in the same way, nor with the same good fortune, as *Esmond*; and there is nothing more to be said on this score. Even if—as always—later researches should have revised our conception of certain of the real personages, the value of the book as an imaginative *tour de force* is unimpaired. Little remains therefore for the gleaner of to-day save bibliographical jottings, and neglected notes on its first appearance.

In Thackeray's work, the place of *The History of Henry Esmond, Esq., a Colonel in the Service of Her Majesty Q. Anne. Written by Himself*—lies midway between his four other principal books, *Vanity Fair, Pendennis, The Newcomes,* and *The Virginians*; and its position serves, in a measure, to explain its origin. In 1848, after much tentative and miscellaneous production, of which the value had been but imperfectly appreciated, the author found his fame with the yellow numbers of *Vanity Fair.* Two years later, adopting the same serial form, came *Pendennis. Vanity Fair* had been the condensation of a life's experience; and excellent as *Pendennis* would have seemed from any inferior hand, its readers could not disguise from themselves that, though showing no falling off in other respects, it drew to some extent upon the old material. No one was readier than Thackeray to listen to a whisper of this kind, or more willing to believe that—as he afterwards told his friend Elwin concerning *The Newcomes*—"he had exhausted all the types of character with which he was familiar." Accordingly he began, for the time, to turn his thoughts in fresh directions; and in the year that followed the publication of *Pendennis,* prepared and delivered in England and Scotland a series of *Lectures upon the English Humourists of the Eighteenth Century.* With the success of these came the prompting for

a new work of fiction,—not to be contemporary,
and not to be issued in parts. His studies for the
Humourists had saturated him with the spirit of a
time to which—witness his novelette of *Barry
Lyndon*—he had always been attracted; and when
Mr. George Smith called on him with a proposal
that he should write a new story for £1,000, he was
already well in hand with *Esmond,*—an effort in
which, if it were not possible to invent new puppets,
it was at least possible to provide fresh costumes
and a change of background. Begun in 1851,
Esmond progressed rapidly, and by the end of May
1852 it was completed. Owing to the limited
stock of old-cut type in which it was set up, its
three volumes passed but slowly through the press;
and it was eventually issued at the end of the following October, upon the eve of the author's departure
to lecture in America. In fact, he was waiting on
the pier for the tender which was to convey him to
the steamer, when he received his bound copies from
the publisher.

Mr. Eyre Crowe, A.R.A., who accompanied
Thackeray to the United States, and had for some
time previously been acting as his "factotum and
amanuensis," has recorded several interesting details
with regard to the writing of *Esmond*. To most
readers it will be matter of surprise, and it is
certainly a noteworthy testimony to the author's

powers, that this attempt to revive the language and atmosphere of a vanished era was in great part dictated. It has even been said that, like *Pendennis,* it was *all* dictated; but this it seems is a mistake, for, as we shall see presently, part of the manuscript was prepared by the author himself. As he warmed to his work, however, he often reverted to the method of oral composition which had always been most congenial to him, and which explains the easy colloquialism of his style. Much of the "copy" was taken down by Mr. Crowe in a first-floor bedroom of No. 16 Young Street, Kensington, the still-existent house where *Vanity Fair* had been written; at the Bedford Hotel in Covent Garden; at the round table in the Athenæum library, and elsewhere. "I write better anywhere than at home,"—Thackeray told Elwin,—"and I write less at home than anywhere." Sometimes author and scribe would betake themselves to the British Museum, to look up points in connection with Marlborough's battles, or to rummage Jacob Tonson's Gazettes for the official accounts of Wynendael and Oudenarde. The British Museum, indeed, was another of *Esmond's* birthplaces. By favour of Sir Antonio Panizzi, Thackeray and his assistant, surrounded by their authorities, were accommodated in one of the secluded galleries. "I sat down,"—says Mr. Crowe—"and wrote to dictation the scathing sentences about the great Marlborough, the denouncing of Cadogan, etc., etc. As a curious instance of literary contagion, it may be here stated that I got quite bitten with the ex- pressed anger at their misdeeds against General Webb, Thackeray's kinsman and ancestor; and that I then looked upon Secretary Cardonnel's conduct with perfect loathing. I was quite delighted to find his meannesses justly pilloried in *Esmond's* pages." What rendered the situation more piquant, —Mr. Crowe adds,—all this took place on the site of old Montague House, where, as Steele's "Prue" says to St. John in the novel, "you wretches go and fight duels."[1]

Those who are willing to make a pilgrimage to Cambridge, may, if they please, inspect the very passages which aroused the enthusiasm of Thackeray's secretary. In a special case in the Library of Trinity College, not far from those which enclose the manu- scripts of Tennyson and Milton, is the original and only manuscript of *Esmond,* being in fact the identical "copy" which was despatched to the press of Messrs. Bradbury and Evans at Whitefriars. It makes two large quarto volumes, and was presented to the College (Esmond's College!) in 1888 by the author's son-in-law, the late Sir Leslie Stephen. It still bears

[1] *With Thackeray in America,* 1893, p. 4.

in pencil the names of the different compositors who set up the type. Much of it is in Thackeray's own small, slightly-slanted, but oftener upright hand, and many pages have hardly any corrections.[1] His custom was to write on half-sheets of a rather large notepaper, and some idea may be gathered of the neat, minute, and regular script, when it is added that the lines usually contain twelve to fifteen words, and that there are frequently as many as thirty-three of these lines to a page. Some of the rest of the "copy" is in the handwriting of the author's daughter, now Lady Ritchie; but a considerable portion was penned by Mr. Eyre Crowe. The oft-quoted passage in book ii. chap. vi. about "bringing your sheaves with you," was written by Thackeray himself almost as it stands; so was the sham *Spectator*, hereafter mentioned, and most of the chapter headed "General Webb wins the Battle of Wynendael." But the splendid closing scene,—"August 1st, 1714,"—is almost wholly in the hand of Mr. Crowe. It is certainly a remarkable fact that work at this level should have been thus improvised, and that nothing,

[1] One is reminded of the accounts of Scott's "copy." "Page after page the writing runs on exactly as you read it in print"—says Mr. Mowbray Morris. "I was looking not long ago at the manuscript of *Kenilworth* in the British Museum, and examined the end with particular care, thinking that the wonderful scene of Amy Robsart's death must surely have cost him some labour. They were the cleanest pages in the volume: I do not think there was a sentence altered or added in the whole chapter" (Lecture at Eton, *Macmillan's Magazine* (1889), lx. pp. 158-9).

as we are credibly informed, should have been before committed to paper.[1]

When *Esmond* first made its appearance in October 1852, it was not without distinguished and even formidable competitors. *Bleak House* had reached its eighth number; and Bulwer was running *My Novel* in *Blackwood*. In *Fraser*, Kingsley was bringing out *Hypatia*; and Whyte Melville was preluding with *Digby Grand*. Charlotte Brontë must have been getting ready *Villette* for the press; and Tennyson—undeterred by the fact that his hero had already been "dirged" by the indefatigable Tupper—was busy with his *Ode on the Death of the Duke of Wellington*.[2] The critics of the time were possibly embarrassed with this wealth of talent, for they were not, at the outset, immoderately enthusiastic over the new arrival. The *Athenæum* was by no means laudatory. *Esmond* "harped upon the same string"; "wanted vital heat"; "touched no fresh fount of thought"; "introduced no novel forms of life";

---

[1] "The sentences"—Mr. Crowe told a member of the Athenæum, when speaking of his task—"came out glibly as he [Thackeray] paced the room." This is the more singular when contrasted with the slow elaboration of the Balzac and Flaubert school. No doubt Thackeray must often have arranged in his mind precisely much that he meant to say. Such seems indeed to have been his habit. The late Mr. Locker Lampson informed the writer of this paper that once, when he met the author of *Esmond* in the Green Park, Thackeray gently begged to be allowed to walk alone, as he had some verses in his head which he was finishing. They were those which afterwards appeared in the *Cornhill* for January 1867, under the title of *Mrs. Katherine's Lantern*.

[2] The Duke died 14th Sept. 1852.

and so forth. But the *Spectator,* in a charming greeting from George Brimley (since included in his *Essays*), placed the book, as a work of art, even above *Vanity Fair* and *Pendennis*; the "serious and orthodox" *Examiner,* then under John Forster, was politely judicial; the *Daily News* friendly; and the *Morning Advertiser* enraptured. The book, this last declared, was the "beau-ideal of historical romance." On December 4 a second edition was announced. Then, on the 22nd, came the *Times.* Whether the *Times* remembered and resented a certain delightfully contemptuous "Essay on Thunder and Small Beer," with which Thackeray retorted to its notice of *The Kickleburys on the Rhine* (a thing hard to believe!) or whether it did not,—its report of *Esmond* was distinctly hostile. In three columns, it commended little but the character of Marlborough, and the writer's "incomparably easy and unforced style." Thackeray thought that it had "absolutely stopped" the sale. But this seems inconsistent with the fact that the publisher sent him a supplementary cheque for £250 on account of *Esmond's* success.

Another reason which may have tended to slacken —not to stop—the sale, is also suggested by the author himself. This was the growing popularity of *My Novel* and *Villette.* And Miss Brontë's book calls to mind the fact that she was among the earliest readers of *Esmond,* the first two volumes of which were sent

M

to her in manuscript by George Smith. She read it, she tells him, with "as much ire and sorrow as gratitude and admiration," marvelling at its mastery of reconstruction,—hating its satire,—its injustice to women. How could Lady Castlewood peep through a keyhole, listen at a door, and be jealous of a boy and a milkmaid! There was too much political and religious intrigue—she thought. Nevertheless she said (this was in February 1852, speaking of vol. i.) the author might "yet make it the best he had ever written." In March she had seen the second volume. The character of Marlborough (here she anticipated the *Times*) was a "masterly piece of writing." But there was "too little story." The final volume, by her own request, she received in print. It possessed, in her opinion, the "most sparkle, impetus, and interest." "I hold," she wrote to Mr. Smith, "that a work of fiction ought to be a work of creation: that the *real* should be sparingly introduced in pages dedicated to the *ideal*." In a later letter she gives high praise to the complex conception of Beatrix, traversing incidentally the absurd accusation of one of the papers that she resembled Blanche Amory [the *Athenæum* and *Examiner,* it may be noted, regarded her as "another Becky"]. "To me," Miss Brontë exclaims, "they are about as identical as a weasel and a royal tigress of Bengal; both the latter are quadrupeds, both the former women." These frank comments of a fervent but thoroughly honest admirer, are of genuine interest. When the book was published, Thackeray himself sent her a copy with his "grateful regards," and it must have been of this that she wrote to Mr. Smith on November 3,— "Colonel Henry Esmond is just arrived. He looks very antique and distinguished in his Queen Anne's garb; the periwig, sword, lace, and ruffles are very well represented by the old *Spectator* type."[1]

One of the points on which Miss Brontë does not touch,—at all events does not touch in those portions of her correspondence which have been printed,—is the marriage with which *Esmond* closes. Upon this event it would have been highly instructive to have had her views, especially as it appears to have greatly exercised her contemporaries, the first reviewers. It was the gravamen of the *Times* indictment; to the critic of *Fraser* it was highly objectionable; and the *Examiner* regarded it as "incredible." Why it was "incredible" that a man should marry a woman seven years older than himself, to whom he had already proposed once in vol. ii., and of whose youthful appearance we are continually reminded ("she looks the sister of her daughter" says the old Dowager at Chelsea), is certainly not superficially obvious. Nor was it obvious to Lady Castlewood's

---

[1] Mr. Clement Shorter's *Charlotte Brontë and her Circle*, 1896, p. 403; and Gaskell's *Life of Charlotte Brontë*, 1900, pp. 561 *et seq.*

children. "Mother's in love with you,—yes, I think
mother's in love with you," says downright Frank
Esmond; the only impediment in his eyes being the
bar sinister, as yet unremoved. And Miss Beatrix
herself, in vol. iii., is even more roundly explicit.
"As for you," she tells Esmond, "you want a
woman to bring your slippers and cap, and to sit at
your feet, and cry 'O caro! O bravo!' whilst you
read your Shakespeares, and Miltons, and stuff"
[which shows that she herself had read Swift's *Grand
Question Debated*]. "Mamma would have been the
wife for you, had you been a little older, though you
look ten years older than she does." "You do, you
glum-faced, blue-bearded, little old man!" adds this
very imperious and free-spoken young lady. The
situation is, no doubt, at times extremely difficult,
and naturally requires consummate skill in the
treatment. But if these things and others signify
anything to an intelligent reader, they signify that
the author, if he had not his end steadily in view,
knew perfectly well that his story was tending in one
direction. There will probably always be some
diversity of opinion in the matter; but the majority
of us have accepted Thackeray's solution, and have
dropped out of sight that hint of undesirable rivalry,
which so troubled the precisians of the early Victorian
age. To those who read *Esmond* now, noting carefully the almost imperceptible transformation of the

motives on either side, as developed by the evolution
of the story, the union of the hero and heroine at
the end must appear not only credible but pre-
ordained.   And that the gradual progress towards
this foregone conclusion is handled with unfailing
tact and skill, there can surely be no question.[1]

Of the historical portraits in the book, the interest
has, perhaps, at this date, a little paled.   Not that
they are one whit less vigorously alive than when the
author first put them in motion; but they have
suffered from the very attention which *Esmond* and
The Humourists have directed to the study of the
originals.   The picture of Marlborough is still as
effective as when it was first proclaimed to be good
enough for the brush of Saint-Simon.   But Thackeray
himself confessed to a family prejudice against the
hero of Blenheim, and later artists have considerably
readjusted the likeness.   Nor in all probability would
the latest biographer of Bolingbroke endorse *that* presentment.   In the purely literary figures, Thackeray
naturally followed the *Lectures,* and is consequently
open to the same criticisms as have been offered on
those performances.   The Swift of *The Humourists,*
modelled on Macaulay, was never accepted from the

---

[1] Thackeray's own explanation was more characteristic than convincing.
"Why did you"—said once to him impetuous Mrs. John Brown of Edinburgh—"Why did you make Esmond marry that old woman?"   "My dear
lady," he replied, "it was not I who married them.   They married themselves."   (*Dr. John Brown,* by the late John Taylor Brown, 1903,
pp. 96-7.)

first; and it has not been accepted in the novel, or by subsequent writers from Forster onwards.[1] Addison has been less studied; and his likeness has consequently been less questioned. Concerning Steele there has been rather more discussion. That Thackeray's sketch is very vivid, very human, and in most essentials, hard to disprove, must be granted. But it is obviously conceived under the domination of the "poor Dick" of Addison, and dwells far too persistently upon Steele's frailer and more fallible aspect. No one would believe that the flushed personage in the full-bottomed periwig, who hiccups Addison's *Campaign* in the Haymarket garret, or the fuddled victim of "Prue's" curtain lecture at Hampton, ranked, at the date of the story, far higher than Addison as a writer, and that he was, in spite of his faults, not only a kindly gentleman and scholar, but a philanthropist, a staunch patriot, and a consistent politician. Probably the author of *Esmond* considered that, in a mixed character, to be introduced incidentally, and exhibited naturally "in the quotidian undress and relaxation of his mind" (as

---

[1] Thackeray heartily disliked Swift, and said so. "As for Swift, you haven't made me alter my opinion"—he replied to Hannay's remonstrances. This feeling was intensified by the belief that Swift, as a clergyman, was insincere. "Of course,"—he wrote in September, 1851, in a letter now in the British Museum,—"any man is welcome to believe as he likes for me *except* a parson: and I can't help looking upon Swift and Sterne as a couple of traitors and renegades . . . with a scornful pity for them in spite of all their genius and greatness."

Lamb says), anything like biographical big drum should be deprecated. This is, at least, the impression left on us by an anecdote told by Elwin. He says that Thackeray, talking to him once about *The Virginians*, which was then appearing, announced that he meant, among other people, to bring in Goldsmith, "representing him as he really was, a little, shabby, mean, shuffling Irishman." These are given as Thackeray's actual words. If so, they do not show the side of Goldsmith which is shown in the last lecture of *The Humourists*.[1]

But although, with our rectified information, we may except against the picture of Steele as a man, we can scarcely cavil at the reproduction of his manner as a writer. Even when Thackeray was a boy at Charterhouse, his imitative faculty had been exceptional; and he displayed it triumphantly in his maturity by those *Novels by Eminent Hands* in which the authors chosen are at once caricatured and criticised. The thing is more than the gift of parody; it amounts (as Mr. Frederic Harrison has rightly said) to positive forgery. It is present in all his works, in stray letters and detached passages. In

---

[1] *Some XVIII. Century Men of Letters*, 1902, i. 187. The intention was never carried out. In *The King over the Water*, 1908, Miss A. Shield and Mr. Andrew Lang have recently examined another portrait in *Esmond*,—that of the Chevalier de St. George,—not without injury to its historical veracity. In these matters, Mr. Lang—like Rob Roy—is on his native heath; and it is only necessary to refer the reader to this highly interesting study.

its simplest form it is to be found in the stiff, circumstantial report of the seconds in the duel at Boulogne in
Denis Duval; and in the missive in barbarous French
of the Dowager Viscountess Castlewood[1]—a letter
which only requires the sprawling, childish script to
make it an exact facsimile of one of the epistolary
efforts of that "baby-faced" Caroline beauty who
was accustomed to sign herself "L duchesse de
Portsmout." It is better still in the letter from
Walpole to General Conway in chap. xl. of *The
Virginians,* which is perfect, even to the indifferent
pun of sleepy (and overrated) George Selwyn. But
the crown and top of these *pastiches* is certainly the
delightful paper, which pretends to be No. 341
of the *Spectator* for All Fools' Day, 1712, in which
Colonel Esmond treats "Mistress Jocasta-Beatrix,"
to what, in the parlance of the time, was decidedly a
"bite."[2] Here Thackeray has borrowed not only
Steele's voice, but his very trick of speech. It is,
however, a fresh instance of the "tangled web we
weave, When first we practise to deceive," that
although this pseudo-*Spectator* is stated to have been
printed "exactly as those famous journals were
printed" for eighteenth-century breakfast-tables, it
could hardly, owing to one microscopic detail, have
deceived the contemporary elect. For Mr. Esmond,
to his very apposite Latin epigraph, unluckily appended

[1] *Esmond,* Book ii. chap. ii.   [2] *Ib.* Book iii. chap. iii.

an English translation,—a concession to the country gentlemen from which both Addison and Steele deliberately abstained, holding that their distinctive mottoes were (in Addison's own phrase) "words to the wise," of no concern to unlearned persons.[1]

This very minute trifle emphasises the pitfalls of would-be perfect imitation. But it also serves to bring us finally to the vocabulary of *Esmond*. As to this, extravagant pretensions have sometimes been advanced. It has been asserted, for instance, by a high journalistic authority, that "no man, woman, or child in *Esmond,* ever says anything that he or she might not have said in the reign of Queen Anne." This is one of those extreme utterances in which enthusiasm, losing its head, invites contradiction. Thackeray professedly "copied the language of Queen Anne,"—he says so in his dedication to Lord Ashburton; but he himself would certainly never have put forward so comprehensive a claim as the above. There is no doubt a story that he challenged Mr. Lowell (who was his fellow-passenger to America on the *Canada*) to point out in *Esmond* a word which had not been used in the early eighteenth century; and that the author of *The Biglow Papers* promptly discovered such a word. But even if the anecdote be not well-invented, the invitation must have been more jest than earnest. For none knew better than

[1] *Spectator*, No. 221, November 13, 1711.

Thackeray that these barren triumphs of wording belong to ingenuity rather than genius, being exercises
altogether in the taste of the Persian poet who left
out all the A's (as well as the poetry) in his verses,
or of that other French funambulist whose sonnet in
honour of Anne de Montaut was an acrostic, a
mesostic, a St. Andrew's Cross, a lozenge,—everything, in short, but a sonnet. What Thackeray
endeavoured after when "copying the language of
Queen Anne," and succeeded in attaining, was the
spirit and tone of the time. It was not pedantic
philology at which he aimed, though he did not
disdain occasional picturesque archaisms, such as
"yatches" for "yachts," or despise the artful aid
of terminal k's, long s's, and old-cut type. Consequently, as was years ago pointed out by Fitzedward
Hall (whose manifest prejudice against Thackeray as
a writer should not blind us in a matter of fact),
it is not difficult to detect many expressions in the
memoirs of Queen Anne's Colonel which could never
have been employed until Her Majesty had long
been "quietly inurned." What is more,—if we
mistake not,—the author of *Esmond* sometimes refrained from using an actual eighteenth-century word,
even in a quotation, when his instinct told him it
was not expedient to do so. In the original of that
well-known anecdote of Steele beside his father's
coffin, in *Tatler* No. 181, reproduced in book i.

chap. vi. of the novel, Steele says, "My mother catched me in her arms." "Catched" is good enough eighteenth-century for Johnson and Walpole. But Thackeray made it "caught," and "caught" it remains to this day both in *Esmond* and *The Humourists*.

A MILTONIC EXERCISE

A MILTONIC EXERCISE

(TERCENTENARY, 1608-1908)

"Stops of various Quills."—LYCIDAS

WHAT need of votive Verse
   To strew thy *Laureat Herse*
With that mix'd *Flora* of th' *Aonian Hill*?
   Or *Mincian* vocall Reed,
   That *Cam* and *Isis* breed,
When thine own Words are burning in us still?

   Bard, Prophet, Archimage!
   In this cash-cradled Age,
We grate our scrannel Musick, and we dote:
   Where is the Strain unknown,
   Through Bronze or Silver blown,
That thrill'd the Welkin with thy woven Note?

   Yes,—we are "selfish Men":
   Yet would we once again
Might see *Sabrina* braid her amber Tire;

Or watch the *Comus* Crew
Sweep down the Glade; or view
Strange-streamer'd Craft from *Javan* or *Gadire*!

Or could we catch once more,
High up, the Clang and Roar
Of Angel conflict,—Angel overthrow:
Or, with a World begun,
Behold the young-ray'd Sun
Flame through the Groves where the *Four Rivers* flow!

.   .   .   .

Ay me, I fondly dream!
Only the storm-bird's scream
Foretells of Tempest in the days to come;
Nowhere is heard up-climb
The lofty lyric Rhyme,
And the "God-gifted Organ-voice" is dumb.[1]

[1] Written by request for the celebration at Christ's College, Cambridge, July 10, 1908.

FRESH FACTS ABOUT FIELDING

FRESH FACTS ABOUT FIELDING

THE general reader, as a rule, is but moderately interested in minor rectifications. Secure in a conventional preference of the spirit to the letter, he professes to be indifferent whether the grandmother of an exalted personage was a "Hugginson" or a "Blenkinsop"; and he is equally careless as to the correct Christian names of his cousins and his aunts. In the main, the general reader is wise in his generation. But with the painful biographer, toiling in the immeasurable sand of thankless research, often foot-sore and dry of throat, these trivialities assume exaggerated proportions; and to those who remind him—as in a cynical age he is sure to be reminded— of the infinitesimal value of his hard-gotten grains of information, he can only reply mournfully, if unconvincingly, that fact is fact—even in matters of mustard-seed. With this prelude, I propose to set down one or two minute points concerning Henry Fielding, not yet comprised in any existing records of his career.[1]

---

[1] Since this was published in April 1907, they have been embodied in an Appendix to my "Men of Letters" *Fielding*; and used, to some extent, for a fresh edition of the *Journal of a Voyage to Lisbon* ("World's Classics").

The first relates to the exact period of his residence at Leyden University. His earliest biographer, Arthur Murphy, writing in 1762, is more explicit than usual on this topic. "He [Fielding]," says Murphy, "went from Eton to Leyden, and there continued to show an eager thirst for knowledge, and to study the civilians with a remarkable application for about two years, when, remittances failing, he was obliged to return to London, not then quite twenty years old" [*i.e.* before 22nd April, 1727]. In 1883, like my predecessors, I adopted this statement, for the sufficient reason that I had nothing better to put in its place. And Murphy should have been well-informed. He had known Fielding personally; he was employed by Fielding's publisher; and he could, one would imagine, have readily obtained accurate data from Fielding's surviving sister, Sarah, who was only three years younger than her brother, of whose short life (he died at forty-eight) she could scarcely have forgotten the particulars. Murphy's story, moreover, exactly fitted in with the fact, only definitely made known in June 1883, that Fielding, as a youth of eighteen, had endeavoured, in November 1725 to abduct or carry off his first love, Miss Sarah Andrew of Lyme Regis. Although the lady was promptly married to a son of one of her fluttered guardians, nothing seemed more reasonable than to assume that

the disappointed lover (one is sure he was never an heiress-hunter!) was despatched to the Dutch University to keep him out of mischief.[1] But in once more examining Mr. Keightley's posthumous papers, kindly placed at my disposal by his nephew, Mr. Alfred C. Lyster, I found a reference to an un-noted article in the *Cornhill Magazine* for November, 1863 (from internal evidence I believe it to have been written by James Hannay), entitled "A Scotchman in Holland." Visiting Leyden, the writer was permitted to inspect the University Album; and he found, under 1728, the following:—
"Henricus Fielding, Anglus, Ann. 20. Stud. Lit.", coupled with the further detail that he "was living at the 'Hotel of Antwerp.'" Except in the item of *"Stud. Lit."*, this did not seem to conflict materially with Murphy's account, as Fielding was nominally twenty from 1727 to 1728, and small discrepancies must be allowed for.

Twenty years later, a fresh version of the record came to light. At their tercentenary festival in 1875, the Leyden University printed a list of their students from their foundation to that year. From this Mr. Edward Peacock, F.S.A., compiled in 1883, for the Index Society, an *Index to English-Speaking Students who have graduated at Leyden University*; and at p. 35 appears *Fielding, Henricus, Anglus,* 16

---

[1] "Men of Letters" *Fielding*, 1907, Appendix I.

Mart. 1728, 915 (the last being the column number of the list). This added a month-date, and made Fielding a graduate. Then, two years ago, came yet a third rendering. Mr. A. E. H. Swaen, writing in *The Modern Language Review* for July 1906, printed the inscription in the Album as follows: "Febr. 16. 1728: Rectore Johanne Wesselio, Henricus Fielding, Anglus. 20, L." Mr. Swaen construed this to mean that, on the date named (which, it may be observed, is not Mr. Peacock's date), Fielding, "aged twenty, was *entered* as *litterarum studiosus* at Leyden." In this case it would follow that his residence in Holland should have come after February 16th, 1728; and Mr. Swaen went on to conjecture that, "as his [Fielding's] first play, *Love in Several Masques,* was staged at Drury Lane in February, 1728, and his next play, *The Temple Beau,* was produced in January, 1730, it is not improbable that his residence in Holland filled up the interval or part of it. Did the profits of the play [he proceeded] perhaps cover part of his travelling expenses?"

The new complications imported into the question by this fresh aspect of it, will be at once apparent. Up to 1875 there had been but one Fielding on the Leyden books; so that all these differing accounts were variations from a single source. In this difficulty, I was fortunate enough to enlist the sympathy of Mr. Frederic Harrison, who most kindly undertook to make inquiries on my behalf at Leyden University itself. In reply to certain definite queries drawn up by me, he obtained from the distinguished scholar and Professor of History, Dr. Pieter Blok, the following authoritative particulars. The exact words in the original *Album Academicum* are:—"16 Martii *1728* Henricus Fielding, Anglus, annor. 20 Litt. Stud." He was then staying at the "Casteel van Antwerpen"—as related by "A Scotchman in Holland." His name only occurs again in the yearly *recensiones* under February 22nd, 1729, as "Henricus Fieldingh," when he was domiciled with one Jan Oson. He must consequently have left Leyden before February 8th, 1730, February 8th being the birthday of the University, after which all students have to be annually registered. The entry in the Album (as Mr. Swaen affirmed) is an *admission* entry; there are no leaving entries. As regards "studying the civilians," Fielding might, in those days, Dr. Blok explains, have had private lessons from the professors; but he could not have studied in the University without being on the books. To sum up: After producing *Love in Several Masques* at Drury Lane, probably on February 12th, 1728,[1] Fielding was admitted a "Litt. Stud." at Leyden University on March 16th; was still there in

---

[1] *Genest*, iii. 209.

February 1729; and left before February 8th, 1730. Murphy is therefore at fault in almost every particular. Fielding did *not* go from Eton to Leyden; he did *not* make any recognised study of the civilians, "with remarkable application" or otherwise; and he did *not* return to London before he was twenty. But it is by no means improbable that the *causa causans* or main reason for his coming home was the failure of remittances.

Another recently established fact is also more or less connected with "Mur.——" as Johnson called him. In his "Essay" of 1762, he gave a highly-coloured account of Fielding's first marriage, and of the promptitude with which, assisted by yellow liveries and a pack of hounds, he managed to make duck and drake of his wife's little fortune. This account has now been "simply riddled in its details" (as Mr. Saintsbury puts it) by successive biographers, the last destructive critic being the late Sir Leslie Stephen, who plausibly suggested that the "yellow liveries" (not the family liveries, be it noted!) were simply a confused recollection of the fantastic pranks of that other and earlier Beau Fielding (Steele's "Orlando the Fair"), who married the Duchess of Cleveland in 1705, and was also a Justice of the Peace for Westminster. One thing was wanting to the readjustment of the narrative, and that was the precise date of Fielding's marriage to the beautiful

Miss Cradock of Salisbury, the original both of
Sophia Western and Amelia Booth. By good
fortune this has now been ascertained. Lawrence
gave the date as 1735; and Keightley suggested the
spring of that year. This, as Swift would say, was
near the mark, although confirmation has been slow
in coming. In June 1906, Mr. Thomas S. Bush, of
Bath, announced in *The Bath Chronicle* that the
desired information was to be found (not in the
Salisbury registers which had been fruitlessly con-
sulted, but) at the tiny church of St. Mary, Charlcombe, a secluded parish about one and a half miles
north of Bath. Here is the record:—"November
yᵉ 28, 1734. Henry Fielding of yᵉ Parish of St.
James in Bath, Esq., and Charlotte Cradock, of yᵉ
same Parish, spinster, were married by virtue of a
licence from yᵉ Court of Wells." All lovers of
Fielding owe a debt of gratitude to Mr. Bush, whose
researches, in addition, disclosed the fact that Sarah
Fielding, the novelist's third sister (as we shall see
presently), was buried, not in Bath Abbey, where
Dr. John Hoadly raised a memorial to her, but "in
yᵉ entrance of the Chancel [of Charlcombe Church]
close to yᵉ Rector's seat," April 14th, 1768.[1] Mr.
Bush's revelation, it may be added, was made in

---

[1] Sarah Fielding's epitaph in Bath Abbey is often said to have been
written by Bishop Benjamin Hoadly. In this case, it must have been
anticipatory (like Dr. Primrose's on his Deborah) for the Bishop died in
1761.

connection with another record of the visits of the
novelist to the old Queen of the West, a tablet
erected in June 1906 to Fielding and his sister on the
wall of Yew Cottage, now renovated as Widcombe
Lodge, Widcombe, Bath, where they once resided.

In the last case I have to mention, it is but fair
to Murphy to admit that he seems to have been
better informed than those who have succeeded him.
Richardson writes of being "well acquainted" with
four of Fielding's sisters, and both Lawrence and
Keightley refer to a Catherine and an Ursula, of
whom Keightley, after prolonged enquiries, could
obtain no tidings. With the help of Colonel W. F.
Prideaux, and the kind offices of Mr. Samuel Martin
of the Hammersmith Free Library, this matter has
now been set at rest. In 1887 Sir Leslie Stephen
had suggested to me that Catherine and Ursula were
most probably born at Sharpham Park, before the
Fieldings moved to East Stour. This must have
been the case, though Keightley had failed to establish
it. At all events, Catherine and Ursula must have
existed, for they both died in 1750. The Hammersmith Registers at Fulham record the following
burials:—

1750 July 9th, Mrs. Catherine Fielding (*sic*)

1750 Nov. 12th, Mrs. Ursula Fielding

1750 [-1] Feby. 24th, Mrs. Beatrice Fielding

1753 May 10th, Louisa, d. of Henry Fielding, Esq.

The first three, with Sarah, make up the "Four Worthy Sisters" of the reprehensible author of that "truly coarse-titled *Tom Jones*," concerning which Richardson wrote shudderingly in August 1749 to his young friends, Astraea and Minerva Hill. The final entry relating to Fielding's little daughter, Louisa, born December 3rd, 1752, makes it probable that, in May, 1753, he was staying in the house at Hammersmith, then occupied by his sole surviving sister, Sarah. In the following year (October 8th) he himself died at Lisbon. There is no better short appreciation of his work than Lowell's lapidary lines for the Shire Hall at Taunton,—the epigraph to the bust by Miss Margaret Thomas:

> He looked on naked nature unashamed,
>   And saw the Sphinx, now bestial, now divine,
> In change and re-change; he nor praised nor blamed,
>   But drew her as he saw with fearless line.
> Did he good service? God must judge, not we!
>   Manly he was, and generous and sincere;
> English in all, of genius blithely free:
>   Who loves a Man may see his image here.

THE HAPPY PRINTER

THE HAPPY PRINTER

"Hoc est vivere."—MARTIAL

THE Printer's is a happy lot:
    Alone of all professions,
No fateful smudges ever blot
    His earliest "impressions."

The outgrowth of his youthful ken
    No cold obstruction fetters;
He quickly learns the "types" of men,
    And all the world of "letters."

With "forms" he scorns to compromise;
    For him no "rule" has terrors;
The "slips" he makes he can "revise"—
    They are but "printers' errors."

From doubtful questions of the "Press"
    He wisely holds aloof;
In all polemics, more or less,
    His argument is "proof."

Save in their "case," with High and Low
　　Small need has he to grapple!
Without dissent he still can go
　　To his accustomed "Chapel."[1]

From ills that others scape or shirk,
　　He rarely fails to rally;
For him, his most "composing" work
　　Is labour of the "galley."

Though ways be foul, and days are dim,
　　He makes no lamentation;
The primal "fount" of woe to him
　　Is—want of occupation:

And when, at last, Time finds him grey
　　With over-close attention,
He solves the problem of the day,
　　And gets an Old Age pension.

---

[1] This, derived, it is said, from Caxton's connection with Westminster Abbey, is the name given to the meetings held by printers to consider trade affairs, appeals, etc. (Printers' Vocabulary).

CROSS READINGS—AND CALEB
WHITEFOORD

CROSS READINGS—AND CALEB
WHITEFOORD

TOWARDS the close of the year 1766—not many
months after the publication of the *Vicar of Wakefield*
—there appeared in Mr. Henry Sampson Woodfall's
Public Advertiser, and other newspapers, a letter
addressed "To the Printer," and signed "PAPYRIUS
CURSOR." The name was a real Roman name; but
in its burlesque applicability to the theme of the
communication, it was as felicitous as Thackeray's
"MANLIUS PENNIALINUS," or that "APOLLONIUS
CURIUS" from whom Hood fabled to have borrowed
the legend of "Lycus the Centaur." The writer
of the letter lamented—as others have done
before and since—the barren fertility of the news
sheets of his day. There was, he contended, some
diversion and diversity in card-playing. But as
for the papers, the unconnected occurrences and
miscellaneous advertisements, the abrupt transitions
from article to article, without the slightest connection between one paragraph and another—so

overburdened and confused the memory that when one was questioned, it was impossible to give even a tolerable account of what one had read. The mind became a jumble of "politics, religion, picking of pockets, puffs, casualties, deaths, marriages, bankruptcies, preferments, resignations, executions, lottery tickets, India bonds, Scotch pebbles, Canada bills, French chicken gloves, auctioneers, and quack doctors," of all of which, particularly as the pages contained three columns, the bewildered reader could retain little or nothing. (One may perhaps pause for a moment to wonder, seeing that Papyrius could contrive to extract so much mental perplexity from Cowper's "folio of four pages"—he speaks specifically of this form,—what he would have done with *Lloyd's,* or a modern American Sunday paper!) Coming later to the point of his epistle, he goes on to explain that he has hit upon a method (as to which, be it added, he was not, as he thought, the originator[1]) of making this heterogeneous mass afford, like cards, a "*variety* of entertainment." By reading the afore-mentioned three columns horizontally and *onwards,* instead of vertically and *downwards* "in the old trite vulgar way," it was contended that much mirth might observingly be distilled from the most

[1] As a matter of fact, he had been anticipated by a paper, No. 49 of "little Harrison's" spurious *Tatler,* vol. v., where the writer reads a newspaper "in a direct Line" . . . "without Regard to the Distinction of Columns,"—which is precisely the proposal of Papyrius.

unhopeful material, as *"blind Chance"* frequently brought about the oddest conjunctions, and not seldom compelled *sub juga aenea* persons and things the most dissimilar and discordant. He then went on to give a number of examples in point, of which we select a few. This was the artless humour of it:—

"Yesterday Dr. Jones preached at St. James's, and performed it with ease in less than 16 Minutes."

"Their R.H. the Dukes of York and Gloucester were bound over to their good behaviour."

"At noon her R.H. the Princess Dowager was married to Mr. Jenkins, an eminent Taylor."

"Friday a poor blind man fell into a saw-pit, to which he was conducted by Sir Clement Cottrell."[1]

"A certain Commoner will be created a Peer. *N.B.*—No greater reward will be offered."

"John Wilkes, Esq., set out for France, being charged with returning from transportation."

"Last night a most terrible fire broke out, and the evening concluded with the utmost Festivity."

"Yesterday the new Lord Mayor was sworn in, and afterwards toss'd and gored several Persons."

"On Tuesday an address was presented; it happily miss'd fire, and the villain made off, when the honour of knighthood was conferred on him to the great joy of that noble family."

"Escaped from the New Gaol, Terence M'Dermot. If he will return, he will be kindly received."

"Colds caught at this season are The Companion to the Playhouse."

---

[1] Master of the Ceremonies.

"Ready to sail to the West Indies,
the Canterbury Flying Machine in one day."
"To be sold to the best Bidder,
My Seat in Parliament being vacated."
"I have long laboured under a complaint
For ready money only."
"Notice is hereby given,
and no Notice taken."

And so forth, fully justifying the writer's motto
from Cicero, *De Finibus: "Fortuitu Concursu hoc
fieri, mirum est."* It may seem that the mirthful
element is not overpowering. But "gentle Dulness
ever loves a joke"; and in 1766 this one, in
modern parlance, "caught on." "Cross readings"
had, moreover, one popular advantage: like the
Limericks of Edward Lear, they were easily imitated.
What is not so intelligible is, that they seem to have
fascinated many people who were assuredly not dull.
Even Johnson condescended to commend the aptness
of the pseudonym, and to speak of the performance
as "ingenious and diverting." Horace Walpole,
writing to Montagu in December 1766, professes to
have laughed over them till he cried. It was "the
newest piece of humour," he declared, "except the
Bath Guide [Anstey's], that he had seen of many
years"; and Goldsmith—Goldsmith, who has been
charged with want of sympathy for rival humourists
—is reported by Northcote to have even gone so
far as to say, in a transport of enthusiasm, that "it

would have given him more pleasure to have been the author of them than of all the works he had ever published of his own,"—which, of course, must be classed with "Dr. Minor's" unconsidered speeches.

"*Bien heureux*"—to use Voltaire's phrase—is he who can laugh much at these things now. As Goldsmith himself would have agreed, the jests of one age are not the jests of another. But it is a little curious that, by one of those freaks of circumstance, or "fortuitous concourses," there is to-day generally included among the very works of Goldsmith above referred to something which, in the opinion of many, is conjectured to have been really the production of the ingenious compiler of the "Cross Readings." That compiler was one Caleb Whitefoord, a well-educated Scotch wine-merchant and picture-buyer, whose portrait figures in Wilkie's "Letter of Introduction." The friend of Benjamin Franklin, who had been his next-door neighbour at Craven Street, he became, in later years, something of a diplomatist, since in 1782-83 he was employed by the Shelburne administration in the Paris negotiation for the Treaty of Versailles. But at the date of the "Cross Readings" he was mainly what Burke, speaking contemptuously of his status as a plenipotentiary, styled a "*diseur de bons mots*"; and he was for this reason included among those "most distinguished Wits of the Metropolis," who, following Garrick's lead in 1774, diverted themselves at the St. James's Coffee-house by composing the epitaphs on Goldsmith which gave rise to the incomparable gallery entitled *Retaliation*. In the first four editions of that posthumous poem there is no mention of Whitefoord, who, either at, or soon after the first meeting above referred to, had written an epitaph on Goldsmith, two-thirds of which are declared to be "unfit for publication."[1] But when the fourth edition of *Retaliation* had been printed, an epitaph on Whitefoord was forwarded to the publisher, George Kearsly, by "a friend of the late Doctor Goldsmith," with an intimation that it was a transcript of an original in "the Doctor's own handwriting." "It is a striking proof of Doctor Goldsmith's good-nature," said the sender, glancing, we may suppose, at Whitefoord's performance. "I saw this sheet of paper in the Doctor's room, five or six days before he died; and, as I had got all the other Epitaphs, I asked if I might take it. *In truth you may, my Boy*, (replied he) *for it will be of no use to me where I am going.*"

---

[1] Hewins's *Whitefoord Papers,* 1898, p. xxvii. n., where the first four lines of twelve are given. They run—

> Noll Goldsmith lies here, as famous for writing
> As his namesake old Noll was for praying and fighting.
> In friends he was rich, tho' not loaded with Pelf;
> He spoke well of them, and thought well of himself.

The lines—there are twenty-eight of them—
speak of Whitefoord as, among other things, a

> Rare compound of oddity, frolic and fun!
> Who relish'd a joke, and rejoic'd in a pun;[1]
> Whose temper was generous, open, sincere;
> A stranger to flatt'ry, a stranger to fear;
> Who scatter'd around wit and humour at will,
> Whose daily *bons mots* half a column would fill;
> A Scotchman, from pride and from prejudice free,
> A scholar, yet surely no pedant was he.
>
> What pity, alas! that so lib'ral a mind
> Should so long be to news-paper-essays confin'd!
> Who perhaps to the summit of science could soar,
> Yet content "if the table he set on a roar";
> Whose talents to fill any station were fit,
> Yet happy if *Woodfall* confess'd him a wit.

The "servile herd" of "tame imitators"—the
"news-paper witlings" and "pert scribbling folks"—
were further requested to visit his tomb—

> To deck it, bring with you festoons of the vine,
> And copious libations bestow on his shrine;
> Then strew all around it (you can do no less)
> *Cross-readings, Ship-news,* and *Mistakes* of the *Press.*

It is not recorded that Kearsly ever saw this in
Goldsmith's "own hand-writing"; the sender's name
has never been made known; and—as above observed

---

[1] "Mr. W."—says a note to the fifth edition—"is so notorious a punster,
that Doctor Goldsmith used to say, it was impossible to keep him company,
without being *infected* with the *itch* of *punning*." Yet Johnson endured
him, and apparently liked him, though he had the additional disqualification
of being a North Briton.

—it has been more than suspected that Whitefoord concocted it himself, or procured its concoction. As J. T. Smith points out in *Nollekens and his Times,* 1828, i. 337-8, Whitefoord was scarcely important enough to deserve a far longer epitaph than those bestowed on Burke and Reynolds; and Goldsmith, it may be added—as we know in the case of Beattie and Voltaire—was not in the habit of confusing small men with great. Moreover, the lines would (as intimated by the person who sent them to Kearsly) be an extraordinary generous return for an epitaph "unfit for publication," by which, it is stated, Goldsmith had been greatly disturbed. Prior had his misgivings, particularly in respect to the words attributed to Goldsmith on his death-bed; and Forster allows that to him the story of the so-called "Postscript" has "a somewhat doubtful look." To which we unhesitatingly say—ditto.

Whitefoord, it seems, was in the habit of printing his "Cross Readings" on small single sheets, and circulating them among his friends. "Rainy-day Smith" had a specimen of these. In one of Whitefoord's letters he professes to claim that his *jeux d'esprit* contained more than met the eye. "I have always," he wrote, "endeavour'd to make such changes [of Ministry] a matter of *Laughter* [rather] than of serious concern to the People, by turning them into horse Races, Ship News, &c., and these

Pieces have generally succeeded beyond my most sanguine Expectations, altho' they were not season'd with private Scandal or personal Abuse, of which our good neighbours of South Britain are realy too fond." In Debrett's *New Foundling Hospital for Wit,* new edition, 1784, there are several of his productions, including a letter to Woodfall "On the Errors of the Press," of which the following may serve as a sample: "I have known you turn a matter of hearsay, into a matter of heresy; Damon into a daemon; a delicious girl, into a delirious girl; the comic muse, into a comic mouse; a Jewish Rabbi, into a Jewish Rabbit; and when a correspondent, lamenting the corruption of the times, exclaimed 'O Mores!' you made him cry, 'O Moses!'" And here is an extract from another paper which explains the aforegoing reference to "horse Races": "1763—Spring Meeting. . . Mr. Wilkes's horse, LIBERTY, rode by himself, took the lead at starting; but being pushed hard by Mr. Bishop's black gelding, PRIVILEGE, fell down at the Devil's Ditch, and was no where." The "Ship News" is on the same pattern. "*August* 25 [1765] We hear that his Majesty's Ship *Newcastle* will soon have a new figure-head, the old one being almost worn out."

THE LAST PROOF

THE LAST PROOF

AN EPILOGUE TO ANY BOOK

"Hic Finis chartaeque viaeque"

"Finis at last—the end, the End, the End!
No more of paragraphs to prune or mend;
No more blue pencil, with its ruthless line,
To blot the phrase 'particularly fine';
No more of 'slips,' and 'galleys,' and 'revises,'
Of words 'transmogrified,' and 'wild surmises';
No more of *n*'s that masquerade as *u*'s,
No nice perplexities of *p*'s and *q*'s;
No more mishaps of *ante* and of *post*,
That most mislead when they should help the most;
No more of 'friend' as 'fiend,' and 'warm' as
        'worm';
No more negations where we would affirm;
No more of those mysterious freaks of fate
That make us bless when we should execrate;
No more of those last blunders that remain
Where we no more can set them right again;

223

No more apologies for doubtful data;
No more fresh facts that figure as Errata;
No more, in short, O TYPE, of wayward lore
From thy most *un*-Pierian fount—NO MORE!"

So spoke PAPYRIUS.   Yet his hand meanwhile
Went vaguely seeking for the vacant file,
Late stored with long array of notes, but now
Bare-wired and barren as a leafless bough;—
And even as he spoke, his mind began
Again to scheme, to purpose and to plan.

There is no end to Labour 'neath the sun;
There is no end of labouring—but One;
And though we "twitch (or not) our Mantle blue,"
"To-morrow to fresh Woods, and Pastures new."

GENERAL INDEX

GENERAL INDEX

[N.B.—*The titles of articles are in capitals*

Addison, Joseph, 8, 34
Adèle et Théodore, 78, 79
Alexandre, Arsène, 103
Allemagne, De l', Mme. de Staël's, 136
Allen, Ralph, 157, 160
Almanacks, Miss Greenaway's, 97, 103
American Notes, Dickens's, 138
Ami des Enfants, Berquin's, 76
A MILTONIC EXERCISE, 191-92
Analysis of Beauty, Hogarth's, 48, 53
Andrew, Sarah, 196
AN EPISTLE TO AN EDITOR, 19-21
Angellier, M. Auguste, 153, 154 *n.*
Anstey, Christopher, 160, 214
A PLEASANT INVECTIVE AGAINST PRINTING, 89
Arable, Mrs. Betty, 114
Art of Politicks, Bramston's, 26, 27
ARTS, M. ROUQUET ON THE, 45-64
As you like it, Caldecott's edition of, 139
Auction of Pictures, 34, 62-63
Austen, Jane, 85, 118-20
A WELCOME FROM THE "JOHNSON CLUB," 165-66
Aynard, M. Joseph, 154 *n.*
Ayscough's *Index to Shakespeare*, 139

Bacon, Francis, 135
Balcöny, or Balcöny, 37-38
Ballad of Beau Brocade, Thomson's, 123
Barbeau, M. A., 154
Barnaby Rudge, Dickens's, 137
Barry Lyndon, Thackeray's, 115 *n.*

BATH, A FRENCH CRITIC ON, 153-62
Bath, A Picture of, 158-62
Batheaston Vase, The, 157
Beljame, Alexandre, 153, 154
Belle-Isle, Marshal Foucquet de, 47, 48
Belles-lettres in 1750, 60
Bentley, Richard, 30, 37
Bewick, Robert Elliot, 7
Bewick, Thomas, 7, 8, 9
Bewick's *Birds and Quadrupeds*, 141
Birthday Book, Miss Greenaway's, 97
Blackmore, Sir Richard, 30
Bleak House, Dickens's, 176
Blenheim, Philips's, 13
Blok, Dr. Pieter, 199
Bloomfield, Robert, 135
Bononcini, C. B., 35
BOOK ILLUSTRATORS, TWO MODERN, 93-104, 111-24
Book of Games, The, Miss Greenaway's, 103
Borough, Crabbe's, 135
Boyle, Richard, Earl of Burlington, 28
Bradshaw, John, 32
Bramston, Francis, 26
Bramston, Rev. James, 25, 26, 29
Bramston, Sir John, the Elder, 26
Bramston, Sir John, the Younger, 26 *n.*
Bramston, Sir Moundeford, 26
BRAMSTON'S MAN OF TASTE, 25-38
Bridgeman, Charles, 33, 49
Brontë, Charlotte, 177-79
Brougham's *Albert Lunel*, 138
Brown, Mr. Ernest, his Thomson book-plate, 120 *n.*
Brown, Mrs. John, 181 *n.*

Brydges, James, Duke of Chandos, 28
Bulmer, William, 8
Bunbury's, H. W., 161
Burchett, Richard, 102
Burford Papers, Hutton's, 157
"Burlington Gate," Hogarth's, 28
Burlington, Lady, 56
Burlington, Richard Boyle, Earl of, 28
Burney, Dr., 134
Burney, Fanny, 79, 121
Bush, Mr. T. S., 201
Butler, Lady, 102
Byron, Lord, 137

Canterbury Tales, Thomson's, 123
Careless Husband, Cibber's, 32
Carlyle's *Cromwell,* 138
Carr, Mr. Comyns, 112, 113
Cervantes, Miguel de, 127
Chandos, James Brydges, Duke of, 28
Chaucer, Bonham's, 140
Chaucer, Geoffrey, 123
Cheere, Sir Henry, 34
Childe Harold, Byron's, 137
Child's Friend, Berquin's, 75
"Child's Song," 101
Cibber, Colley, 32, 37
Cibber, Gabriel, 57
Clennell, Luke, 142
Coaching Days and Coaching Ways, Outram Tristram's, 115
Cochin, Charles Nicolas, 46, 49, 64
Columbus, Rogers's, 142
Comic Writers, Lectures on The, Hazlitt's, 15
Compleat Angler, The, 6, 71
Coplas, Manrique's, 13
Coram, Captain Thomas, 10
Coridon's Song, etc., Thomson's, 120, 121
Corinne, Mme. de Staël's, 136
Courier, P. L., 30
Courthope, Mr. W. J., 165
Coverley, Sir Roger de, 113, 114
Cowley, Abraham, 146
Crabbe, George, 135
Cradock, Charlotte, 201
Cranford, Mrs. Gaskell's, 85, 117, 118
Cranford Series, 120, 121
Cranford, Thomson's, 117, 118, 121
Crooked Sixpence, The, Bramston's, 27
CROSS READINGS—AND CALEB WHITEFOORD, 211-19

Crowe, Mr. Eyre, 172, 173, 174, 175, 176 n.
Crowe, William, 139, 143

Dance of Death, Holbein's, 141
Danton, the caricaturist, 145
Dassier, Anthony, 58
Davy, Sir Humphry, 136
Day in a Child's Life, A, Miss Greenaway's, 97, 99
Day, Thomas, 77, 79
Days with Sir Roger de Coverley, Thomson's, 113
Decameron, Boccaccio's, 141
Delphine, Mme. de Staël's, 136
Derocquigny, M. Jules, 154 n.
Dickens, Charles, 132, 133, 137, 138
Diderot, Denis, 57
Digby Grand, Whyte Melville's, 176
Dispensary, Pope's copy of Garth's, 139
Diversions of Purley, Horne Tooke's, 141
"DON QUIXOTE," HORATIAN ODE ON THE TERCENTENARY OF, 127-28
Douady, M. Jules, 154 n.

Eastlake, Lady, 146
Edgeworth, Maria, 71-86, 123
Edgeworth, Mr., 76, 78, 82 n.
EDITOR, AN EPISTLE TO AN, 19-21
Eliot, George, 121
Elwin, Rev. Whitwell, 171, 173, 183
English Illustrated Magazine, 112, 114
Enquiry into Polite Learning, Goldsmith's, 31
Ephraim the Quaker, 114
Esmond, Thackeray's, 169-87
Esmond, Thomson's, 121, 123
État des Arts, Rouquet's, 45-64
Evelina, Thomson's, 121
Evelyn, John, 156 n.
Evenings at Home, Dr. Aikin's, 75

Fairie Queene, Spenser's, 140
Farmer's Boy, Bloomfield's, 135
Ferrier, Miss Susan, 85
Fielding, "Beau," 200
FIELDING, FRESH FACTS ABOUT, 195-203
Fielding, Henry, 160; his stay at Leyden, 196-200; his marriage, 200-1; his sisters, 202-3

Fielding, Sarah, 196, 201, 203
Fielding, The Misses, 202
Fiennes, Celia, her Diary, 156
Figg, the prize-fighter, 37
"Finding of Moses," Hogarth's, 52
Fitzgerald, Mr. Percy, 132, 133 n.
Flaxman, John, 134.
Foote, Samuel, 47
Fox, Charles James, 15, 36
Franklin, Benjamin, 215
FRENCH CRITIC ON BATH, A, 153
FRESH FACTS ABOUT FIELDING, 195-203
FRIEND OF HUMANITY AND THE RHYMER, THE, 67-68
Furniss, Mr. Harry, 113

Gardelle, Theodore, 47
Gardening, Landscape, 33, 49
Gardens of Adonis, 37
Garrick, David, 47, 61, 131
Gaskell, Mrs., 117
Gay, John, 165
"Ginevra" (Italy), 137
Goldsmith, Cunningham's, 14, 15
Goldsmith, Oliver, 31, 35 n., 37, 157, 183, 214
"Good Samaritan," Hogarth's, 53
Gosse, Mr. Edmund, 145 n.
Goupy, Joseph, 56
Grammont's Memoirs, 157
Gray, Thomas, 31
GREENAWAY CHILD, A SONG OF THE, 107
Greenaway, John, 102
Greenaway, Kate, 93-104, 123

"Hagar and Ishmael," Highmore's, 52
Hall, Fitzedward, 186
Halsewell, Loss of the, 144
Hamlet, Caldecott's edition of, 139
Handel, 56
Hannay, James, 197
Hanway, Jonas, 62
Harrison, Mr. Frederic, 183, 198
Harrison's Tatler, 212 n.
Harry and Lucy, Edgeworth's, 79
Hayman, Francis, 52, 54
Hazlitt, W., 15, 138
Hazlitt's Criticisms on Art, 138
Highmore, Joseph, 52, 54
Highways and Byways series, 122
Highways and Byways of London Life, Cook's, 122
History of Life and Death, Bacon's, 7
History Painting, 50-54
Hoadly, Dr. John, 201

Hoare of Bath, William, 140
Hogarth, Mrs., 12
Hogarth's "Man of Taste," 28
Hogarth, William, 11, 28, 34, 35, 50, 51, 52, 53, 54, 64, 113
Holcroft, Thomas, 79
Homer, Cowper's, 143
HORATIAN ODE ON THE TERCENTENARY OF "DON QUIXOTE," 127-8
Huchon, M. René, 154 n.
Hudson, Thomas, 54
Hugo, Victor, 117
Huntingdon, Lady, 157, 160
Hurd, Bishop, 160
Hutton, Dr. Charles, 9
Hypatia, Kingsley's, 176
Hypnerotomichie of Poliphilus, 141

"In an Apple-Tree," 101
Ireland, John, 48
Ireland, Samuel, 12, 13
Ireland, William Henry, 12

Jerrold, Douglas, 111
"JOHNSON CLUB," A WELCOME FROM THE, 165-6
Johnson, Samuel, 31, 82, 214
Johnson, Joseph, the publisher, 73-76
Jones, Inigo, 33
Jordan, Mrs., 161
Jusserand, M. J.-J., 153

Kate Greenaway's Painting Book, 103
Kearsly, George, 216, 217, 218
Keightley, Thomas, 197, 201, 202
Kent, William, 28, 49, 50
Kentucky Cardinal, Allen's, 121
Kickleburys on the Rhine, Thackeray's, 177
King over the Water, Shield's and Lang's, 183 n.
King Pepito, Miss Greenaway's, 103
Kneller, Sir Godfrey, 54

Labelye, Charles, 46, 60
Lalla Rookh, Moore's, 137
La Motte, M., 161
Lampson, F. Locker, 38, 99, 132, 176
Landor, W. S., 13, 169 n.
Lang, Mr. Andrew, 113, 183 n.
Langley, Batty, 33
Language of Flowers, Miss Greenaway's, 103
Lansdowne, Marquess of, 137
Layard, Mr. G. S., 29, 104

"Lazy Lawrence," Miss Edgeworth's, 81

Leake, James, 160

Le Blanc, Abbé, 55 *n.*, 57

Lee, Mr., 161

Legouis, M. Émile, 154

Legros, Prof., 102

Lessons for Children, Mrs. Barbauld's, 75

Letters to Literary Ladies, Miss Edgeworth's, 80

Lewesdon Hill, Crowe's, 143

Leyden University, Fielding at, 196-200

Linley, Elizabeth, 157

Liotard, J. S., 46

Little Ann, Miss Greenaway's, 97, 99

"Little Nell," Dickens's, 137

Locker, Frederick, *see* Lampson

Locker, Lampson portraits, 100

Loffт, Capel, 135

London and Wise, Messrs., 50

Longfellow's *Ballads,* 138

Longfellow's *Voices of the Night,* 138

Lowell, James Russell, 185, 203

Lusiads, Camoens's, 141

Lyrics of the Heart, A. A. Watts's, 15

Lyster, Mr. Alfred C., 197

Macaulay's *Lays,* 138

Maclise, Daniel ("Alfred Croquis"), 143

Maginn, William, 145

Mandeville, Bernard de, 32

Man of Taste, Bramston's, 25-38

Man of Taste, Hogarth's, 28

Manzoni's *Promessi Sposi,* 143

Marianne, Marivaux's, 142

Marigny, Abel-François Poisson, Marquis de, 45, 46, 49, 64

Marigold Garden, Miss Greenaway's, 97, 100, 104

Martin, Mr. Samuel, 202

Master Humphrey's Clock, 132, 137

Melmoth, William, 160

Memoirs Relating to the Royal Navy, Pepys', 10

Mensuration, Hutton's, 9

Metamorphoses d' Ovide, Renouard's, 4

Meteyard, Miss Eliza, 111

Miller, Lady, 157

Milton, John, 31, 140, 143

Milton Tercentenary, 1608-1908, 191

MILTONIC EXERCISE, A, 191-2

Missionary, Bowles's, 136-7

Mistakes of the Press, 217, 219

Mitford, Miss, 117

Monamy, Peter, 56

Montagu, Mrs., on Shakespeare, 139

Montaigne, Michel de, 31 *n.*

Moore, Edward, 135

Moore, Thomas, 137

Moral Essay, No. 4, Pope's, 28

Morel, M. Léon, 154

Morris, Mr. Mowbray, 175 *n.*

Moser, Michael, 46, 47, 64

"Moses brought to Pharaoh's Daughter," Hogarth's, 52

Mourning Bride, Congreve's, 25

M. ROUQUET ON THE ARTS, 45-64

Murphy, Arthur, 52 *n.*, 196, 200

"Musing," 103

My Novel, Bulwer's, 176, 177

Nash, Richard, 157

Newspaper, The Eighteenth Century, 58-60

Nicholas Nickleby, Dickens's, 137

Nivernais, Duc de, 50

Nollekens and his Times, Smith's, 218

North Briton, The, 11, 12

Northcliffe, Lord, 134 *n.*

Old Curiosity Shop, Dickens's, 137

Oldfield, Mrs., 32

"Old Poz," 80, 86

"Omnium, Jacob," 30

ON SOME BOOKS AND THEIR ASSOCIATIONS, 3-15

Paine, Edmund (Rogers's servant), 142

Pamela, Richardson's, 142

Panizzi, Sir Antonio, 173

"Papyrius Cursor," 211

Paradise Lost, Milton's, 140

PARENT'S ASSISTANT, THE, 71-86

Passeran, Count, 33

PASSIONATE PRINTER TO HIS LOVE, THE, 41-42

"Paul before Felix," Hogarth's, 53

Peacock, Mr. Edward, 197

Peg Woffington, Thomson's, 121

Peinture en Cire, Diderot's, 63

Peinture en Fromage, L' Art nouveau de la, Rouquet's, 63

Pennell, Mr. Joseph, 124

PEPYS' "DIARY," 149-50

Pepys, Samuel, 9, 156

Philips, John, 13

Pied Piper of Hamelin, 97

Pilgrim of Glencoe, Campbell's, 138

Pilgrim's Progress, Bunyan's, 72
PLEASANT INVECTIVE AGAINST PRINTING, A, 89
Pleasures of Memory, Rogers's, 132, 142
Pompadour, Jeanne-Antoinette Poisson, Marquise de, 46
"Pool of Bethesda," Hogarth's, 53
Pope, Alexander, 15, 28, 32, 139
Porteus, Bishop, 160
Portrait in oil, 54-56
Prestongrange, Lord, 14
Prideaux, Col. W. F., 202
Procter, Mrs., 146
PROOF, THE LAST, 223
Pursuits of Literature, Mathias's, 8

Queen of the Pirate Isle, Bret Harte's, 97
Quin, James, 161

Rabbe, M. Felix, 153
Racine, *Mémoires* of, by his son, 143
Railton, Mr. Herbert, 115
Ramsay, Allan, 55
Rauzzini, Venanzio, 161
Reade, Charles, 121
Retaliation, Goldsmith, 216
Reynolds, Sir Joshua, 134, 141
Richardson, Samuel, 160, 203
Rimbault, Dr., 10
Ritchie, Lady, 83, 175
Rogers, Samuel, 38
ROGERS, SAMUEL, THE BOOKS OF, 131-46
Rose and the Ring, The, Thackeray's, 82
Roubillac, L. F., 57
Rouquet, Jean-André, 45-64
ROUQUET, M., ON THE ARTS, 45-64
Rousseau, Jean-Jacques, 143
Ruskin, John, 96, 103
Ruxton, Miss Sophy, 75
Rysbraek, J. M., 57

Sanford and Merton, Day's, 79
Scenes of Clerical Life, Thomson's, 121
Scheemakers, Thomas, 57
"Scotchman in Holland, A," 197
Scott, Samuel, 56
Scott, Sir Walter, 84, 137, 175 *n.*
Seymour, James, 56
Sheridan, R. B., 136, 157
Ship News, 217, 219
Shorter, Mr. Clement, 179 *n.*
Shovel, Sir Cloudesly, 34
Siddons, Mrs., 161

Silas Marner, Thomson's, 121
"Simple Susan," Miss Edgeworth's, 74, 85
Sketches by Boz, Dickens's, 133
Smith, J. T., 218
Smith, Mr. George, 172, 179
Solly, Prof. Edward, 10
SONG OF THE GREENAWAY CHILD, A, 107
Southey, Robert, 13
Spielmann, Mr. Marion H., 104 *n.*
Spiritual Quixote, Graves's, 157
Splendid Shilling, Philips's, 13, 27
Staël, Mme. de, 136
Standly, H. P., 11, 12
Stapfer, M. Paul, 153
"Stareleigh, Mr. Justice," 132
St. Bruno, Le Sueur's, 141
Steele, Sir Richard, 183-4, 186
Steevens, George, 47
Stephen, Sir Leslie, 174, 202
Sterne, Laurence, 182 *n.*
Stevenson, R. L., 14
St. James's Palace, No. 22, 132, 134
Story of Rosina, Thomson's, 123
Stothard, Thomas, 93-4, 123, 134
"Suffer Little Children," Wills's, 52
"Sun Door, The," 100
Sure and Certain Method of Attaining a Long and Healthy Life, Cornaro's, 7
Sussex, Dallaway and Cartwright's, 27
Swaen, Mr. A. F. H., 198, 199
Swift, Jonathan, 30, 182 *n.*
Sylva Sylvarum, Bacon's, 6
Symmons, Samuel, the Printer, 140

Taine, Hippolyte, 153
Tales from Maria Edgeworth, Thomson's, 123
Tales of the Hall, Crabbe's, 135
"Tarleton," Miss Edgeworth's, 81
Tar Water, Bishop Berkeley's, 77
Taste, Of False, Pope's, 28
Taste, Of, Pope's, 28
Tatler, Harrison's, 212 *n.*
Talyor, Isaac, 99
Taylor, Jane and Ann, 99
Thackeray's *Esmond,* 169-87
Thackeray, W. M., 121, 169-87
THE BOOKS OF SAMUEL ROGERS, 131-46
"The False Key," Miss Edgeworth's, 81, 83
THE FRIEND OF HUMANITY AND THE RHYMER, 67-68

"THE HAPPY PRINTER," 207-8
THE LAST PROOF, 223-4
"The Mimic," 81, 82, 84
THE PARENT'S ASSISTANT, 71-86
Thomas, Miss Margaret, 203
Thomas, M. W., 154
Thomson, James, 14, 31, 154
THOMSON, MR. HUGH, 111-24
Tennyson's Ode on the Death of
    the Duke of Wellington, 176
Tennyson's Poems, 138
Texte, Joseph, 154, 156
"Time Smoking a Picture," Ho-
    garth's, 51
Tindal, Matthew, 32
Tom Jones, Fielding's, 36
Tooke, Horne, 140, 141 n.
Traill, H. D., 113
Trinity College, Cambridge, 174
Trollope, Anthony, 169
Tutor's Assistant, The, 76
TWO MODERN BOOK ILLUSTRATORS,
    93-104, 111-24
Tyers, Jonathan, 61

Under the Window, Miss Green-
    away's, 103
Use of Riches, On the, Pope's, 28

Vails-Giving, 62
Vanbrugh, Sir John, 33
Vandergucht, Gerard, 29
Vanhaken, Joseph, 55, 56
Vanloo, Jean-Baptiste, 55
Vauxhall in 1750, 61
Vicar of Wakefield, Thomson's, 116
Villette, Charlotte Brontë's, 176, 177
Vortigern and Rowena, W. H. Ire-
    land's, 13

Walpole, Horace, 49, 50, 57, 214
Watts, Alaric A., 14
Whitbread, Samuel, 136
Whitefield, George, 160
Whitefoord, Caleb, 215-19
WHITEFOORD, CALEB, AND CROSS
    READINGS, 211-19
Whitefoord Papers, Hewins's, 216 n.
Wilkes, John, 11
Wilkie, David, 215
Wimble, Will, 114
Woodfall, Henry Sampson, 211
Wootton, John, 56
Wordsworth's Poems, 138
Wren, Sir Christopher, 33

Zincke, Christian, 47, 56, 57, 64

THE END

Anthologies of Varied Charm Collected by E. V. LUCAS

The Gentlest Art

A Choice of Letters by Entertaining Hands

An anthology of letter writing, so human, interesting, and amusing from first to last, as almost to inspire one to attempt the restoration of a lost art. "We do not believe that a more likable book has been published this year."—*The Evening Post, Chicago.*

Cloth, 12mo, viii + 240 pp., $1.25 net.

Another Book of Verse for Children

Verses of the seasons, of "little fowls of the air" and of "the country round"; ballads of sailormen, and of battle; songs of the hearthrug, and of the joy of being alive and a child, selected by Mr. Lucas and illustrated in black and white and with colored plates by Mr. F. D. Bedford. The wording of the title is an allusion to the very successful *Book of Verse for Children* issued ten years ago. The *Athenæum* describes Mr. Lucas as "the ideal editor for such a book as this."

Cloth, 8vo, col. illus., $1.50 net.

The Ladies' Pageant

Better than any one else whose name comes to mind, Mr. Lucas has mastered the difficult art of the compiler. There is more individuality in *The Gentlest Art*, for instance, than in the so-called original works of many an author. This happy knack of assembling the best things in the world on a given subject is given free play in the present book, the subject of which is the Eternal Feminine. Here are all the best words of the poets on a theme which surely offers scope for more variety than any other within the view of the reader. Like others of Mr. Lucas' books, this is attractively bound and decorated.

Cloth, 12mo, $1.25 net.

Character and Comedy

The Tribune: "Of all the readers of Charles Lamb who have striven to emulate him, Mr. Lucas comes nearest to being worthy of him. Perhaps it is because it is natural to him to look upon life and letters and all things with something of Lamb's gentleness, sweetness and humor."

Cloth, 16mo, viii + 239 pp., $1.25 net.

Published by

THE MACMILLAN COMPANY

Sixty-four and Sixty-six Fifth Avenue
NEW YORK